Sporting Peugeot 205s

Sporting Peugeot 205s

A collector's guide
by Dave Thornton

MOTOR RACING PUBLICATIONS LTD
Unit 6, The Pilton Estate, 46 Pitlake, Croydon CR0 3RY, England

First published 1997

British Library Cataloguing in Publication Data

Thornton, Dave
    Sporting Peugeot 205s : a collector's guide
    1. Peugeot automobile – Collectors and collecting 2. Sports
    cars – Collectors and collecting
    I. Title
    629.2'222

ISBN 1-899870-19-9

Printed in Great Britain by
The Amadeus Press Ltd
Huddersfield, West Yorkshire

Cover picture:
A Peugeot 205 GTI 1.9, once the author's own car, shown with a Zender bodykit and Peugeot Talbot Sport grille stripes.

Contents

Introduction and acknowledgements		Tools, cycles and coffee grinders	6
Chapter 1	In the beginning	A new class of car	9
Chapter 2	Peugeot 205 GTI 1.6	A new class of car	13
Chapter 3	205 GTI 1.9	If you want something sensible – buy an anorak	25
Chapter 4	Other sporting 205s	The Lion goes from strength to strength	33
Chapter 5	205 GTI special editions	Adding exclusivity to substance	49
Chapter 6	205 Cabriolets	Two cars in one	59
Chapter 7	205 Turbo 16	"Sir, we have won"	71
Chapter 8	The 205 in motorsport	Rallies, races and raids	87
Chapter 9	Ownership and modifications	Getting the best out of your 205	95
Appendix A	Technical specifications		122
Appendix B	Production milestones		124
Appendix C	Sales figures in the UK		125
Appendix D	Useful addresses		125
Appendix E	Performance figures for 205s		128

Introduction and acknowledgements

The introduction of the Peugeot 205 in 1983 signalled one of the biggest changes of fortune in the history of the motor industry. The success of this model has transformed Peugeot from a manufacturer of staid, but reliable saloon and estate cars into a company that has won the World Rally Championship, the Paris-Dakar rally and the Le Mans 24-hours race and nowadays plays an important role in Formula One and Touring Car racing.

The concept of the 205, or M24 as it was known whilst on the drawing-board, was surprisingly simple: a small five-door car. The Peugeot 104 and its siblings, the Talbot Samba and Citroen Visa, were not hard acts to follow, so it was easy for the 205 to make quantum leaps in style, technology, packaging, performance and economy. Its major competitor was the Renault 5, which had been the best-selling small car in France for many years.

The Peugeot 205 was designed to have a big-car feel and so to appeal to motorists who were downsizing. It was already a success before the launch of the sportier three-door versions that this book deals with, but it was the launch of the 205 T16 rally car in 1983, followed by the 205 GTI in 1984, which changed Peugeot's image forever.

A new class of car was born – a fuel-injected 1.6 or 1.9-litre engine in a supermini – and the motoring press could not praise it highly enough. Many motoring journalists chose it as their personal transport, and in 1990 it was voted by one leading magazine as 'Performance Car of the Decade', citing its achievement as bringing performance motoring to the masses.

It is both a pleasure and a privilege to be the author of a *Collector's Guide* for such an entertaining series of cars, models which if anything have proved to be more popular than ever since 1994, when all but a few of the 205 derivatives ceased production. After having written the magazine of the Peugeot Sport Club for over seven years and owned four 205 GTIs and a 205 CTI over a 10-year period, I trust I am sufficiently well qualified to convey my enthusiasm and knowledge of this wonderful car to you. There is something special and magical about a car that begs to be driven and is universally liked, especially one which is within the grasp of everyday folk; you're reading about such a car now.

It was difficult to draw the line as to which models should be included and which should be passed over. For example, should the book encompass all the 205 derivatives, or should it, perhaps, include all of Peugeot's ever-expanding range of performance models? We hope the term 'sporting 205s' accurately reflects the choice we have made, believing that these are the models for which there is the greatest and most widespread enthusiasm, which is not to say, of course, that the 205 Junior, or the diesel and van derivatives, are not all fine pieces of machinery in their own right. Where possible, sporting derivatives that were not sold in the UK have also been included.

Inevitably, this book could not have been written without the assistance and encouragement of others, and indeed these people are so numerous that it is not possible to thank them all individually both for their help in providing information and technical advice, and for maintaining my enthusiasm and brand loyalty over a 10-year period. Colin Lewis and the team in the Public Relations Department at Peugeot have been particularly useful in piecing together the history of the 205, and as a result of my involvement with the owners' club, which began in 1989, a number of people have enhanced my interest in the marque by sharing information, releasing cars for test drives and providing editorial contributions and photographs for the club's magazine *Torque*. Therefore, I must record my thanks to Tony Munday and the plethora of Peugeot Sport Club officers and members over the years, to Des O'Dell, Mick Linford, Keith Baud and the team at Peugeot Sport in Coventry, and to Alan Ranger, Gordon Jarvis, Richard Burns, Patrick O'Donovan, David Oldham, Terry Pankhurst, Graham Mitchell, Mike Shonfield and Danny Rota, to name but a few, not forgetting members of my family. Finally, I must mention Alec Davis, without whom I would have had no information about the T16.

I cannot stress too strongly that joining the Peugeot Sport Club, or one of its many equivalents in Europe, is the best way to maximize your enjoyment of the car. The hints and tips, discounts and insurance scheme available will save the average person the cost of membership many times over. The activities of the club are covered in more detail in Chapter 9.

My observations have convinced me that, though the standard car is excellent, most enthusiasts will want to personalize their car, either mechanically or visually, and therefore I have explained in considerable detail the magnitude of tuning options available.

I was persuaded to buy a 205 GTI 1.6 in 1987 by the favourable comments the model had received in the press and by the image it was building. I had also been impressed by seeing the finale of the 1986 RAC rally in Bath, won by a 205 T16, a car which demonstrated so convincingly that performance had been engineered rather than added on. The image has never dimmed, and despite the harsh insurance climate in the early 1990s, the models have remained extremely popular. No other manufacturer has brought quality performance motoring to the masses in this country so effectively in recent years, and none has succeeded in injecting so much fun into that performance.

If you think that a car is all about getting from A to B, then you haven't driven a sporting 205. If you don't already own one, I hope this book will inspire you to do so; and if you already have one, I hope you will be encouraged to continue the enjoyment of driving it for many more years to come.

June 1997   DAVE THORNTON

CHAPTER 1

In the beginning

Tools, cycles and coffee grinders

We can trace the ancestry of Peugeot back to 1810 when two Peugeot brothers, Jean-Pierre and Jean-Frederic, transformed a windmill into a small factory to make tools and springs. This expanded throughout the 19th century, and by 1882 they had produced their first bicycle and were making items as diverse as coffee grinders.

Peugeot tried their luck with a steam-powered tricycle, but it was very heavy and, in 1890, the first Peugeot car, the Type 2, was manufactured, powered by a twin-cylinder Daimler engine. The various derivatives of Peugeots were named by the prefix Type, followed by a number. The last of these was the Type 190 in the late 1920s, before the launch of the Peugeot 201 in 1929.

The motorsport heritage, which reached such a pinnacle in the Eighties, started as early as 1895 when a Type 3 won the Paris-Bordeaux-Paris race. In 1914, Peugeot No 14 lapped Indianapolis at an average speed of 76mph, with a top speed of 118mph. This car was well ahead of its time, having a 3-litre, four-cylinder, 16-valve DOHC engine.

Robert Peugeot took over the company in 1910, and in 1926 he rationalized its production facilities, separating the car division from other activities. The launch of the 201 had introduced a new trend in model identification, and in due course many three-figure numbers, with a zero for the middle digit in the 101 to 909 range, were to be registered so that no other manufacturer could use them. This certainly caught out Porsche, who in 1963 had to hastily rename their intended new 901 and call it the 911.

By 1935, a comprehensive range had been developed with the 201, 301, 401 and 601 models. The success of these carried Peugeot through the leaner years of the depression, and in late 1935 they launched the 402, with aerodynamic bodywork, which was quite something for the time. By 1938, diesel and automatic variants were also being offered, but the imminent war hampered their development.

In 1936, a Peugeot dealer from Paris, Darl'Mat, became involved in races and making roadster versions of the 302 and 402, the latter winning the 2-litre category of the 1938 Le Mans 24-hours race. A year later a similar model broke the world land speed record for its class by reaching 124mph.

During the war, the Peugeot factories, being so close to the German border, were commandeered to produce military equipment under the supervision of Volkswagen. However, when the war ended, Peugeot bounced back quickly and the new 203 was ready for launch in 1948; nearly 700,000 examples of this car in many guises would be sold by 1960. A larger model, the 403, was launched in 1955 and, under the guidance of the Italian body designer Pininfarina, a convertible was introduced soon after. Incidentally, Pininfarina is still instrumental in the styling of Peugeot's coupes and convertibles.

The numerical predecessor of the 205 was launched in 1965. The 204 had front-wheel drive and an alloy transversely-mounted engine, which was a first for Peugeot. Then in 1968 the legendary 504 was introduced, providing the platform for a string of rally victories in Africa during the 1970s.

This Peugeot 203 from the mid-Fifties has been prepared for Historic saloon car racing.

Peugeot took over Chrysler's European subsidiaries in 1978 and renamed their models under the Talbot banner. They also became more active in motorsport, their Matra division powering the Ligier Formula One car in 1981, while the Lotus-powered Talbot Sunbeam won the World Rally Championship in 1980 in the hands of the late Henri Toivonen.

Amongst Peugeot's production cars, there were no predecessors to the sporting 205s at the beginning of the Eighties save for the tiny 104S (five-door) and 104 ZS (three-door) hatchbacks with 1.4-litre engines and alloy wheels. Interestingly, however, a much-facelifted and more sporting version of the three-door 104 was offered in the form of the Talbot Samba. Produced between 1979 and 1985, a Rallye version was also offered, which was an ideal

base for a rally car and was also produced as a cabriolet. This remained in production, by Pininfarina in Italy, until 1986, when the 205 CTI began to be assembled at the same factory.

In the early Eighties, the badging policy for Peugeots had been to identify their models as GL, GR, GT, etc, the engines of which were all carburettor-fed. However, the 2.2-litre engine that powered the 505 and 505 Estate was fuel-injected, as a result of which these models were given the designation 505 GTI. It was only logical, therefore, that when the fuel-injected version of the 205 was introduced, it too would be a GTI; the model badging was certainly not a deliberate copy from Volkswagen, who had created the first 'hot hatch' in 1975 and called it a GTI. And so the legendary 205 GTI was born ...

The GTI's immediate predecessors in the Peugeot range were the sporting versions of the 104, the 104ZS (three-door) and the 104S (five-door). Engines and transmissions were carried over from the 104 for the lower powered versions of the 205.

The Musee Peugeot in Sochaux has Peugeots on display from the 1890s to the 1990s, including this quartet of Peugeot 203s, 403 saloon and 404 saloon.

The shop at Musee Peugeot is probably the Mecca for Peugeot enthusiasts, with the lion motif and Peugeot logos available on a very wide range of merchandise and regalia.

Musee Peugeot

In 1988, the history of Peugeot was preserved forever with the opening of Musee Peugeot, a museum in Sochaux, France, dedicated entirely to the world of Peugeot. There are exhibits which mirror the company's history from the beginning of tool production right through to the present day. Most of the car models are represented, and there is also an area for cycles, motorcycles and mopeds, plus an historic garage. Competition cars are also well-represented, including 205 T16s and 405 T16s from the World Rally Championship and Paris-Dakar rallies. The Peugeot 905 that won Le Mans in 1991 was installed in the entrance hall and there are further mock-ups. A film is regularly shown about the history of Peugeot and there is a shop to purchase all sorts of regalia, clothing and models, all with the distinctive Peugeot logo and lion.

Visitors to the museum who arrive at 8.30am on weekdays may also take a trip to the nearby Sochaux factory to see new cars in production. The entrance fee is very reasonable and the museum is signposted from the A36 autoroute with brown signs. Musee Peugeot, Carrefour de l'Europe, 25600 Sochaux. Tel: (00 33) 81 94 48 21.

CHAPTER 2

Peugeot 205 GTI 1.6

A new class of car

The launch of the 205 GTI was probably the most radical model announcement for Peugeot of the postwar era because it precipitated a fundamental image change, and in company with a chain of events in motorsport it has altered the marque's presence in the marketplace irreversibly. The change was already under way by February 1983 with the announcement of the 205 range, which replaced the ageing 104 and gave Peugeot something with which to compete squarely against the Renault 5 that had dominated the sales charts in France. The announcement coincided with the company's declaration of intent to enter the World Rally Championship with a derivative of the same model.

When the 205 Turbo 16 rally car was unveiled it looked remarkably similar to the roadgoing 205 models, but in fact it shared very little with its lesser brothers. Although the 205 was already a commercial success without the motorsport influence, there is little doubt that the marque's image transformation would not have taken place without the GTI. Later in the life of the 205, the 205 Turbo 16 became history when Group B rally cars were banned at the end of 1986, and thereafter the GTI took sole responsibility for the sporting aspirations of Peugeot.

In September 1983, the 205 range went on sale in the UK with a range of five-door models in four specification levels (base, GL, GR and GT). Diesel variants of the GL and GR were known as GLD and GRD, but the GT was the quickest model, with a twin-carburettor 1,360cc engine producing 79bhp at 5,800rpm. The only sporting clues on this distinctly sporting model were a discreet spoiler, GT badging and stickers on the front wings.

However, this would not be the top model for long, and the GT badge became GTI with the introduction of a 1.6-litre, 105bhp, fuel-injected engine. It was to be a model that sat awkwardly against the competition. Half a class above were cars like the VW Golf GTI (which had just grown with the advent of the Golf 2), Ford's Escort XR3i and the Vauxhall Astra GTE. Below were the 1.3-litre turbocharged MG Metro Turbo and the normally-aspirated 1.6-litre Ford Fiesta XR2. The new Peugeot had the performance of the larger cars with the smaller size of the latter.

The 205 GTI's dimensions were not too different from those of the original – and at the time definitive – hot hatch, the Golf GTI Mk 1. So, the class had been established, but there was a gap in the market.

When launched, the model also seemed to fit uncomfortably in the showrooms. The dealer networks of Peugeot and Talbot (*nee* Chrysler) had been merged and the 205 GTI sat alongside models such as the Talbot Horizon and Solara. Peugeot's 305 and 604 were also from a different era.

Advertising was a key factor in the impending image change. On paper the 205 GTI appeared alongside a roadgoing version of the 205 Turbo 16 and looked surprisingly similar to it, intentionally of course. Peugeot deliberately copied the style of the alloy wheels and the body decals to give the GTI more credibility as a sporting car. It worked a treat. On the billboards the Peugeot's lion symbol became more prominent as slogans read: 'A

An early 205 GTI 1.6, pictured with its larger brother, the 405, just visible behind it. Note the design of the Speedline wheels, which are similar to those on the 205 Turbo 16.

The handling and poise of the 205 GTI are exemplary, as displayed here at Donington Park, with a 1.9 version in hot pursuit.

The 205 GTI was an instant hit in Peugeot showrooms, and when designed it was intended to be the only three-door 205 model.

constructor shows its claws' and the now famous '*Un Sacre Numero*' appearing wherever the 205 appeared. It didn't quite translate as 'a sacred number', more 'what a number!', which epitomized the car. In France, '*deux cents cinq*' rolled off every tongue as if it had been a part of gallic life for years.

On the screen, however, was a different story that eventually backfired. So intent was the company on creating a youthful appeal, the theme chosen for the television commercial was a spoof James Bond plot. Filmed on location in the Kalahari desert, a speeding GTI dodged exploding landmines, narrowly missed an express train and more significantly outran a chasing helicopter firing rockets. Finally, the car dived off a cliff and landed safely by parachute, the driver adjusting his bow tie and carrying on as if nothing had happened. There was only one call of dissent, from Aerospatiale, whose Gazelle helicopter (which was capable of 185mph) had been shown in a very poor light. The helicopter manufacturer complained to the French Government on the grounds that it could be an own

goal for their arms business, so the advert, which had cost Peugeot millions of francs, was withdrawn.

The GTI, initially intended as a low-volume model in a niche market, was to be the only three-door 205, but a year later a complete range of X-series 205s went on sale as a slightly cheaper alternative to the five-door variants. However, there was never any likelihood of a five-door GTI; in particular, the bodykit would not have worked around the rear wheelarches, which were designed differently, being larger on GTI bodyshells.

April 1984 saw the first 205 GTIs being sold in the UK. A press launch had taken place on the windy mountain roads in Southern Spain, where the car had immediately impressed the journalists, who loved its pin-sharp handling, although they were less enamoured with its harsh ride. Given that one of Peugeot's traditional strengths was ride quality, this was something of a disappointment, but it was acknowledged as the cost of great advances in handling. *Autocar* concluded that the 205 GTI had "the strongest claim to date to be considered the legitimate successor to

the late, lamented Mini-Cooper S".

It was launched with a 1,580cc XU5J fuel-injected, belt-driven overhead-camshaft engine developing 105bhp at 6,250rpm. Maximum torque of 99lb.ft was achieved at 4,000rpm and a rev-limiter cut in at 6,500rpm. Peugeot claimed that the car was capable of 118mph, with 0-60mph taking 9.1 seconds. Despite being a performance car, its generous power-to-weight ratio resulted in excellent economy. At a constant 56mph, 50.4mpg was achievable, with 38.7mpg at a steady 75mph and 32.5mpg on the urban cycle. The engine was mounted transversely and mated to the side-mounted BE-1 five-speed close-ratio gearbox, in which fifth was a 'short' ratio, not a true overdrive. Reverse was obtained by lifting a collar around the gear-lever and moving the lever to the left and forwards.

The suspension was slightly different on the GTI, having been engineered rather than just adjusted, like most of its competitors. At the front were MacPherson struts with coil springs and an anti-roll bar. At the rear was an ingenious set-up which was designed to have minimal intrusion into the boot space. It had a cross-tube with trailing arms, torsion bars, shock absorbers (inclined at 30 degrees) and an anti-roll bar. The ride height was 17mm lower than on the other models. The contact with the road was through 5.5J-14 Speedline 12-hole alloy wheels, which had been modelled on those from the Turbo 16. They were unusual in not having a hole in the centre and consequently they have proved difficult to balance. The tyres were 185/60HR-14 and cars left the factory shod in either Michelin MXV or Pirelli P600 rubber.

A performance car should be equipped with an uprated braking system and the GTI was to be no exception, with the provision of ventilated front discs of 247mm diameter and drum brakes at the rear. A larger servo was fitted to the GTI model, although not for the right-hand-drive models. The handbrake worked on the rear drums. A two-stage thermostatically controlled electric fan was deployed to help keep the tight engine bay cool, and the radiator was topped up by means of an expansion tank at the rear of the engine bay.

The dashboard on the GTI models is slightly different from that on the rest of the range and contains a rev-counter and both oil pressure and temperature gauges as part of its comprehensive instrumentation. This 1987 model has a leather-rimmed steering wheel.

The facelift in 1988 was accompanied by a new dashboard layout, including rotary heater controls, and the 1.6 GTI had tweed upholstery instead of the previous velour.

A 50-litre (11-gallon) fuel tank was much larger than in the average supermini of the mid-Eighties and this took four-star petrol (or 95 RON unleaded after a dealer adjustment), fed into the engine by a Bosch LE2-Jetronic fuel-injection system. Steering was by rack and pinion and 3.8 turns lock to lock gave a turning circle of 32.6ft.

Buyers of the first 205 GTIs had a choice of white, red, black, Silver or Graphite Grey as a body colour, which came with Biarritz velour seat trim and matching black front head restraints. Interestingly, the choice of black or metallic paint cost no extra on the original £6,245 price tag. All of these colours enhanced the look that Peugeot had created specially for the GTI. At the front, twin long-range driving lamps were mounted in a deeper front spoiler and the

bumpers had a bright red insert. Along the side of the car, wide grey mouldings continued the theme of the bumpers, and the C-pillar had twin decals announcing '1.6' and 'GTI', with the fuel filler cap incorporated on the right-hand side.

Twin door mirrors were fitted to right-hand-drive models, and though the mirrors were smaller and of a sporty design, the curvature of the lens more than compensated, and they proved to be better in practice. They were adjustable from the inside with a small knob mounted on each door. Such attention to detail helped the car to achieve a class-leading drag coefficient of just 0.34, against 0.35 for the rest of the 205 range. A long wheelbase on a short car only enhanced its purposeful looks and made the car very desirable. Only

Accommodation for front-seat passengers is particularly good, thanks to minimal front wheelarch intrusion and a sensible range of seat adjustment. Storage is adequate, too, with generous doorbins, a lockable glovebox and recesses on the top of the facia.

six months later, demand for it had made it easy for the price to be increased to £6,645 and 1,874 GTIs had been registered in Great Britain by the end of the first year.

To match the velour seat trim, which was black with red pinstriping, Peugeot chose to follow the style of the MG Metro and Maestro and fitted red carpets. These really enhanced the inside of the car, but they proved none too practical. The standard equipment was not outstanding, but all GTIs came with a stereo radio/cassette player and four speakers, bronze tinted glass and a rear wash/wipe. Options included a sliding glass sunroof, which was initially on the options list at £165, and a combined option of central locking of doors and tailgate and front electric windows at £353.

Instrumentation was particularly comprehensive for this category of car. Apart from the speedometer and rev-counter, there were supplementary gauges for fuel level, water temperature, oil pressure and oil temperature. The usual array of warning lights was on display through the centre of a two-spoke steering wheel, which had a padded centre containing the GTI lettering. In the centre console was the Phillips radio/cassette and heater controls. To say the least, the heating and ventilation performance was something of an Achilles' heel, with an inability to provide that cool-head, warm-feet scenario as well as offering very poor-quality demisting. The fan could not be turned off, either, because it was required to give a small flow of air to aid demisting, but this proved more irritating than its worth.

Accommodation was a strong feature of the 205 GTI. The body was 12ft 2in long, which made it the largest in the supermini class at the time. It was also the first supermini to have a 'big car' feel, and the driver and passenger sat in sports seats, quite high up, but not so high as to provide poor headroom. Unlike many of its competitors, front wheelarch intrusion was minimal, which enabled the pedals to be right in front of the driver, not set to the left. Rear seat passengers were also given a good deal. The front seats tipped forward to allow generous access to the 50/50 split/folding rear seat. These were soft but comfortable. A smallish boot (7.6cu ft) was a good shape, thanks to minimal suspension intrusion, which opened up to a cavernous 42.4cu ft with both seats folded flat.

It didn't take long, though, for Peugeot to make adjustments to the suspension. In February 1985, the GTI was made with softer settings to provide a better ride, with little being lost in the handling department. The model proved so popular that in May 1985 the marketing department at Peugeot decided to launch a dedicated owners' club, the Peugeot 205 GTI Club, more of which in Chapter 9. By the end of 1985 the press were really warming to the car, and a further 4,971 UK registrations were made. In total, nearly 85,000 GTI models had left the production line deep in the Forest of Harth, near Mulhouse, in the south-east of France, close to the Swiss border.

But despite such success, the competition was beginning to hot up. Renault had introduced the 5 GT Turbo, which had a 115bhp 1.4-litre engine, and the Fiat Uno Turbo ie produced a similar figure. A small amount of competition had also emerged from within the ranks as the corporate Peugeot-Citroen parts bin supplied the Citroen Visa with the same 105bhp engine as well as the front suspension for the Visa GTI. But despite this model's dynamic ability, it never sold in great numbers, which went to prove how important were the 205's looks and image to its manufacturer. This same image had such an effect that company car drivers were demanding the 205 GTI instead of similarly priced versions of cars like the Vauxhall Cavalier and Ford Sierra.

The target bhp figure for the uprated 1.6 XU5JA engine that appeared in 1986 had already been defined by Renault with the GT Turbo. Peugeot were able to match this by making alterations to the cylinder head, and fitting a new camshaft with increased valve lift and overlap, and larger valves. The engine was also revised in other ways to cope with the additional power, including thicker cylinder block liners, strengthened connecting rods, new big-end and main bearings, and new valve guides and springs. The magical 115bhp was developed at 6,250rpm, but torque was unchanged at 98.4lb.ft at 4,000rpm. Performance was improved, top speed now being a claimed 121mph, with a 0-60mph time of 8.9 seconds. As might be expected, fuel economy suffered, 47.9mpg being recorded at a constant 56mph, 37.7mpg at a steady 75mph and 30.7mpg on the urban cycle, meaning a drop of around 2mpg for the average driver.

Two visible clues to a post-June 1986 model are side repeater indicators and a leather-bound steering wheel, of the same design as the original. The instrument graphics were much clearer, too, with fewer lines and smaller numbers. The column stalks were changed cosmetically and the feed for the washer bottle was altered. Previously, a very large reservoir was located in the left-hand front wheelarch, which served the windscreen and the back window via tubing, whereas the rear now had its own bottle in the right-hand side of the boot. As safety factors became more dominant (and the law changed), Peugeot decided it was time to fit three seat belts in the rear (two inertia, one lap).

The external mirrors were redesigned and enlarged, with large adjusting handles on the interior; the entire mirror adjusted, not just the glass. But despite the increased mirror area, the field of view was not improved, and if the mirror was knocked it had to be repositioned whereas the old mirrors would spring back.

Sales increased month by month and, despite the introduction of the CTI and, in December 1986, the 1.9-litre version of the GTI, the 1.6 was now established as one of the top sellers in the 205 range. Buyers of the original 105bhp model were trading them in for the more powerful version, such was their popularity.

In January 1988 the entire 205 range underwent its most significant revision. New engines and trim were introduced for the lower range models, but the 205 GTI 1.6, as it was now known, gained the new 205 dashboard and new Monaco tweed seat trim. This was a harder-wearing trim that was much better able to withstand the pressure on the seat's thigh supports, which deformed and looked messy on the earlier Biarritz-trimmed models. The facia was a completely new design, a higher quality plastic being used. The heater controls were positioned higher and were now of a rotary rather than a sliding type, and the fan could be

The boot is a good size at 7.6cu ft, and with the rear suspension slanted at 30 degrees there is no intrusion of the struts into the boot area, which therefore can be much wider than on other cars in its class.

With one seat folded there is room for three passengers and a reasonable quantity of luggage.

switched off completely. On the top of the dashboard was a coin tray with a lid. The downside was the centre console, which still had the radio/cassette positioned very low, and the clock was now beside the ashtray and totally obscured from the driver's view by the steering wheel on right-hand-drive models. The space for cassettes was also slightly smaller. The steering wheel was now an elegant three-spoke design with the 'GTI' lettering in red in the centre, while the column stalks were revised again to a round design, and the door trims now extended to the base of the windows, minimizing the amount of bare metal in the car.

Metallic paint had become an extra-cost option, the same five colours still being available. Externally, the major change was a modified tailgate design, which can be identified by a straight-lipped rear spoiler that doesn't curve around the window at the top. Mechanically, the car was unchanged.

In September 1989, a '1990 model' GTI 1.6 was launched, the biggest mechanical change being the adoption of the BE-3 gearbox, recognizable by the position of reverse

– back right. Cosmetically, the seat trim was now Quartet velour in black and red, with plain black velour side supports. This combination appeared simultaneously in the revised 309 GTI and suited the red carpets perfectly. The boot area was carpeted for the first time. Earlier in 1989, Peugeot had produced a new range of stereo equipment in conjunction with Clarion and the VAR9318 model was fitted to all GTI models. Previously on the options list, central locking was now standard, and if the optional electric windows were selected, the switches were illuminated.

The price had risen to £9,835, which could be increased further with the options of sliding glass sunroof (£215), electric windows (£242), metallic paint (£144), black paint (£113) or, new for 1990, power-assisted steering (£350). A limited-edition model was shown in October 1989 at Motorfair in London's Earls Court, but this model is covered in Chapter 5. During 1990, the 205 GTI was also available for a short time with light blue metallic paintwork, called Topaz Blue, but this was soon discontinued.

Just 12 months later, Peugeot freshened the appearance of the 205 range with black bumpers and mouldings, crystal clear front indicators and a new style of rear lens. The brake lights and tail-lights had been separated and the reversing light had been relegated to a single light in the rear valance. Internally, the plastic on the doors and the facia had also darkened, making it a better match for the seat trim. The specification was upgraded to include a lights-on warning buzzer and remote operation of the central locking. Anti-lock braking became an option for the first time (£600) and a standard car now cost £10,695, while the price of other options had increased by around 10 per cent. Additionally, pearlescent paint was now available at £196 in Sorrento Green, while Miami Blue and Steel Grey metallic were also introduced. Sorrento Green and Steel Grey had black-and-green Quartet velour and a dark green carpet instead of the red.

Laser Green was introduced during 1991, with the same interior as the Sorrento Green models, but the colour was soon dropped, becoming available only on the newly

Peugeot always produced specialist brochures for the GTI models because they were so distinctive from the other cars in the range.

introduced 106 models. There were no further changes to the 1.6 GTI, and with the law allowing only catalyst-equipped models to be sold from 1993, this model disappeared from the Peugeot range in October 1992.

Driving impressions
My first 205 GTI was a 105bhp model from 1985, an original car, just two years old, with black paintwork and rock-hard suspension! I was encouraged by the press reports and I also liked the idea of a 1.6-litre fuel-injected engine in a small car. Peugeot had made the largest supermini to date, and it certainly felt like driving a much bigger car. The 14in wheels helped that feeling, as did the commanding driving position. I decided it was £5,000 well spent.

When a child, I was always impressed by top speeds and 0-60mph acceleration times, like most car fanatics of that age.

But it was the handling of my first Peugeot that made me realize that roadholding and cornering ability, as well as braking, were the real keys to performance motoring. After all, our roads were too congested and twisting to appreciate straight-line speed. The gearbox and its close ratios also played a part in my enjoyment of this car and its high-revving engine – a power unit that would rev quite happily from tickover to the limiter at 6,500rpm. The car was as happy at 30mph in fifth as at 75mph in third!

With 105bhp, the car was no slouch, in fact it was much quicker than the Ford Fiesta XR2 (96bhp) and the MG Metro Turbo (93bhp) that were being made at the same time. Its handling was good because the 205 could 'talk' through the steering wheel and, above all, it was fun. Many journalists have subsequently commented that the 205 GTI 1.6 is a car you could drive for the sheer hell of it, just to enjoy the drive; I couldn't agree more. Long journeys

Many owners of early GTIs fitted this red reflective tailgate panel, which was available as a dealer accessory.

weren't tiresome, just extended pleasure.

Although essentially a driver's car, its accommodation was equally agreeable for passengers. Legroom was generous and the front passenger's seat, though hard, was comfortable, while rear seat passengers had softer but equally comfortable seat cushions. Storage, which included a central cubbyhole and two large door bins, was also good, and the boot was a useful shape. All of my passengers liked the car, and one even bought a 205 GTI having enjoyed a foreign trip as a passenger so much.

It was also a sensible performance car to own. Servicing was minimal, especially as nothing went wrong, except for the usual stalling problems and a replacement exhaust at 42,000 miles. Insurance was in the old group 5 (now 12), which was not too extortionate in 1987, and – most surprisingly – fuel economy was excellent. After 20,000 miles the average was over 34mpg, with a best figure of nearly 43mpg on the aforementioned foreign trip. I sold the car for just £500 less than I had paid for it. I had enjoyed the 1.6 GTI so much I had decided to buy a 1.9 version!

CHAPTER 3

205 GTI 1.9

If you want something sensible – buy an anorak

To launch a better and faster GTI model when the present model was top of the class showed the measure of success Peugeot was enjoying with the 205 GTI. From December 1986 until the end of 1992, two variants of the 205 GTI were available in the UK. The 1.9 version was one of a select few cars to have been produced without any direct competition – except, of course, its less powerful brother. One could argue that the nearest match was Peugeot's own 309 GTI, with the same engine, or perhaps Ford's Escort RS Turbo and Volkswagen's Golf GTI 16-valve, both of which were more expensive.

For a premium of around £1,000 (the initial price was £9,295), buyers were being offered electric windows and central locking as standard, half-leather seats with Quattro velour centre panels, and 15in Speedline alloy wheels with 185/55VR-15 tyres. These were the visible clues to the new model, but mechanically the differences were also marked. Beneath the bonnet lay a 1,905cc version of the XU engine, the XU9JA. Gear ratios were adjusted, with a particularly high first giving 6.2mph per 1,000rpm, which meant a theoretical maximum speed in first gear of 43mph, and a similarly high second gear capable of propelling the car to 68mph; this took account of the 130bhp and 119lb.ft of torque, as did the extra size of the wheels and tyres. To stop the car, the front ventilated discs were retained, but paired with solid discs at the rear. There was a small weight increase, but even so, performance figures of 7.6 seconds from 0 to 60mph and a top speed of 127mph were highly impressive.

Advertising

Advertising played a key part in the image of the 1.9 version. However, the T16 links that launched the 1.6 GTI were now only applicable in the brochures as Group B rallying had been banned at the time of the launch, so it was no longer appropriate for use in magazine adverts. So a silver 1.9 GTI appeared on a rooftop at night-time with the slogan: 'Hot Cat on a Tin Roof'. The adverts appeared later with the caption: 'If you want something sensible – buy an anorak'. With the September 1990 revision, at a time when Peugeot was truly supreme in the hot hatch market, the message read: 'Wolf in Wolf's Clothing'. During 1992 and 1993, selling GTIs of any description was difficult, but Peugeot continued to market the 1.9 strongly, with a Miami Blue version demonstrating the 'old-fashioned crafts' of weaving (superior handling), wood-turning (roadholding) and taxidermy (stuffing the opposition).

Short supply

At launch, models were increasingly hard to come by, and orders were rolling in from customers who had never previously bought a Peugeot in addition to those wishing to trade up from a 1.6 to a 1.9. This phenomenon continued throughout the car's life and brand loyalty was immense. A substantial proportion of customers who eventually found the 205's size too small for their needs bought another car from the Peugeot range, notably the 309 GTI (with the same engine as the 205 GTI 1.9) and (from 1988) the 405 Mi16, with a 160bhp 16-valve version of the same 1,905cc engine.

A 1987 GTI 1.9 in Graphite Grey. It can be identified as a pre-1988 model by its rear spoiler. The 15-inch alloy wheels fill the arches perfectly.

At its peak the 205 GTI accounted for over 20 per cent of all 205 sales in the UK. Note how the factory-fitted sliding sunroof compares with the tilting sunroof fitted to the nearer car.

Incidentally, Peugeot were not the first to offer a 1.9-litre version of their GTI. Tuning companies such as Skip Brown Cars and Chartersport offered conversions to convert a 1.6 engine into a 1.9, with a similar output of 130bhp, a full 12 months earlier than the factory, and later, the tuning companies were not short of business tuning the larger engine. The chapter on ownership and modifications explains the potential of both engines.

The standard 1.9, like the 1.6, was available at launch with a choice of Alpine White, Cherry Red, Silver, Graphite Grey or black paint, and had the option of a sliding sunroof. It seemed, though, that most cars left the factory in either white or red (the only colours that did not cost extra), and cars without the optional sunroof were hard to come by. Its first specification change came with the January 1988 facelift, where the new dashboard and revised tailgate and spoiler were fitted. At the beginning of 1989, the stereo equipment was changed from Phillips to Clarion, and a minor revision in August 1989 heralded the the new BE-3 gearbox, with reverse positioned to the right and back,

whereas before it was to the left and forward, with the use of a protective collar to prevent it being selected by accident. A slightly bigger exhaust tailpipe became standard, but there was no noticeable increase in power. This minor revision also marked the gradual change of the interior colours, with the introduction of new seat trim – black half-leather with black and red Quartet velour centre panels. The electric window switches also became illuminated. For a period of nearly a year, Topaz Blue metallic became an option, although surprisingly few cars were produced in this colour.

At the 1989 Motorfair at Earls Court, Peugeot made a catalytic converter an optional extra on the 1.9 engine for an additional £350. However, customers did not wish to pay the extra for an option that gave the car a reduced output of 122bhp from the XU9JAZ engine (against a true 128bhp of the normal car) and reduced performance figures of 125mph top speed and 0-62mph in 8.5 seconds. Economy was worse, too, although the 'cat'-equipped engine could run on 95 RON unleaded fuel. However, the

Pininfarina styled the Convertible version of the 205, but the 1.9 badge also made the car very attractive. Unfortunately, these badges themselves have become a target for mindless vandals.

This 1989 GTI 1.9 sports the Quattro velour seats with leather side rolls. The light grey of the driver's seat, however, would show dirt very easily.

The bright carpet also tends to show dirt easily and it is best protected by a set of four tailored carpet mats.

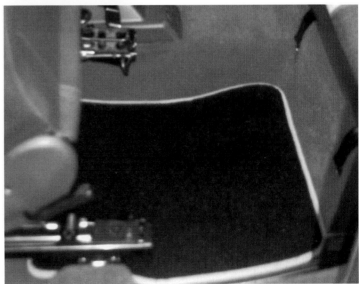

introduction of 98 RON super unleaded fuel meant that the standard car could be run on this without alteration.

One of the few drawbacks of the 1.9 was its heavy steering, and the power-assisted steering that appeared on the limited-edition models in 1990 was made an option in September 1989, with anti-lock braking appearing as an option from September 1990. There were also some new colours: the Miami Blue metallic and pearlescent Sorrento Green that appeared on the limited-edition cars, and Steel Grey metallic, a lighter shade than the Graphite Grey. The latter two colours went with black half-leather seats with green-and-black Quartet velour centre panels and very tasteful dark green carpets. This was the time when the front indicator lenses became clear, the rear lenses were redesigned (including a single reversing light in the rear valance), and the plastics used for the bumpers, door trims and dashboard all changed to black.

The only changes in 1991 were the introduction of a very bright Laser Green metallic paint which, like the Topaz Blue, was only available for around 12 months, and the

The new dashboard on post-1988 models was accompanied by this attractive three-spoke leather-rimmed steering wheel.

introduction of remote-control central locking by means of a hand-held keypad. Although the model was beginning to show its age, its biggest accolade was announced when *Performance Car* magazine voted the 205 GTI 1.9 its 'Performance Car of the Decade', for bringing performance car motoring to the masses.

At the end of 1992, with sales dwindling rapidly due to the colossal increase in insurance premiums, the 1.6 was deleted from the range and the 1.9 was thereafter only available with the catalysed 122bhp engine. The red carpet was substituted with grey, and air conditioning became an option. Power-assisted steering was now standard and a keypad immobilizer/alarm appeared on final versions. The model was available 'only whilst stocks last' from October 1993, so most of the last cars were registered in early 1994, although the very last of all had an 'M' registration, which was introduced on August 1 that year.

By this time, Peugeot had launched two sporting versions of the 106 (XSi and Rallye) and two of the 306 (XSi and S16). In terms of size, the 205's true replacement would

In September 1989 Peugeot replaced the Quattro velour with the Quartet variety and a year later the interior plastic went from grey to black, as shown on this 1991 GTI 1.9.

The 15-inch Speedline alloy wheels are nothing short of beautiful, but they require care and attention when parking to avoid damage and should be cleaned regularly to remove brake dust and salt in winter. Models from 1989 onwards were fitted with slightly larger side repeater indicators.

not arrive until the launch of the 206 range, but increasingly stringent safety and emissions regulations dictate that a car as light and as powerful as the 1.9 GTI will probably never appear again. That said, the 106 GTI (known as the 106 S16 in France), which was launched at the end of 1996, comes tantalizingly close.

Driving impressions

I have owned two 1.9 GTIs: a 1987 model in Graphite Grey and a white car from 1989. The most noticeable difference from the 1.6, apart from the interior specification and an extra 15 or 25bhp, comes from the use of the larger-diameter wheels. There are pros and cons to this: manoeuvring is harder, but roadholding is much greater. Cornering limits are higher, although the manner in which

In August 1990, along with darker bumpers and trim, clear front indicator lenses improved the frontal aspect of the 205 and can be retro-fitted to all 205s.

the rear end of the 1.6 can step out during heavy cornering is more gradual. The hidden benefit of having larger-diameter rims is the ability to fit disc brakes all round, which is essential in a car with 130bhp.

Although the engine may be more powerful, it was not as sweet as the 1,580cc unit, nor was it as free-revving. This is a property of a long-stroke engine like the 1.9, whereas the

1.6 was slightly ove-rsquare. The free-revving ability was further compromised by the gearing chosen, first and second gear ratios being appreciably higher on the 1.9. However, with such a good power-to-weight ratio, the car would still fly. With over 40mph available in first gear and nearly 70mph in second, the 1.9 was the quickest hot hatch away from the lights. Its 0-60mph time was quickest, too, as a result of this close-ratio gearing.

With the use of half-leather, the interior was harder-wearing as well as more attractive, adding a touch of luxury to the car. The electric windows and central locking were reliable, and I found maintenance costs to be similar to those for the 1.6 version. Insurance was two groups higher at group 14, and fuel consumption was around 2mpg heavier, but these were still comparatively cheap cars to run, because of their lowish depreciation.

Keeping the 1.9 engine in perfect tune is no easier than the 1.6, but it can be helped by using injection cleaner and having the engine serviced by a mechanic who genuinely knows the workings of the fuel injection, butterfly valve, airflow meter and supplementary air device (cold start device).

The performance abilities of the 1.9 are very high, but even the best cars can be improved. Rather like the feelings I experienced when I craved for a 1.9 whilst owning a 1.6, it is hard to ignore the modifications available to make the 1.9 go even faster ...

The 205 GTI 1.9 was voted by *Performance Car* magazine as 'Performance Car of the Decade' in 1990.

Many owners are intent on keeping their pride and joy in tip-top condition and entering *Concours d'Elegance* competitions. Note the cleanliness of the exhaust silencer.

There were only a few hundred GTI 1.9s sold in 1993, and this pristine example is sure to be an appreciating asset as one of the last to be produced, especially with this registration mark to complement it.

CHAPTER 4

Other sporting 205s

The Lion goes from strength to strength

205 Rallye

It was a great shame that the 'real' 205 Rallye was only built in left-hand-drive form and hence never appeared in the UK other than as a personal import for rallying use. The model was homologated for rallying in the up-to-1,300cc class, in which it proved highly effective. The showroom model owed much of its specification to its rallying heritage.

Launched in 1988, and deleted at the end of 1992, this model could be interpreted as a cut-price GTI, but it certainly had its own character. Priced around 15 per cent less than a 1.6 GTI, it was powered by a 103bhp 1,294cc engine equipped with two twin-choke Weber carburettors. Coupled with low gearing, this high-revving engine propelled the car to a top speed of 118mph and from 0-60mph in around 9 seconds. Peak power was developed at 6,800rpm (with a rev-limiter set at 7,100rpm) and peak torque was produced at 5,000rpm. Many components were borrowed from the GTI models, including the brakes, suspension, front and rear spoilers and the seating.

The external paintwork (available only in white initially) and the Peugeot Talbot Sport (PTS) stripes on the front grille and tailgate complemented the special colour-coded wheelarch extensions and the white-painted steel wheels. The driving lamp holes in the front spoiler were replaced by brake cooling vents. The only alteration to the model's external appearance during its lifespan was the change to the later-style front and rear light lenses, a modification which affected the whole range in September 1990.

The interior specification could only be described as sparse, but at the same time it was in keeping with the character of the model, and aimed at keeping weight to a minimum – just 1,738lb. With no electrical goodies, door trim short of the window sills, only a two-speaker radio/cassette and no sunroof, the interior was more akin to an entry-level 205 than a GTI, but it did have the GTI's seating and steering wheel. The seats were trimmed in plain black velour, similar to the side supports of the Biarritz velour found on the early 1.6 GTIs, and the PTS logo appeared on the centres of the backrests and the steering wheel.

On the continent, the Rallye was to become an ideal clubman's rally car, and of the few imported to the UK, it proved surprisingly successful in the Peugeot Rally Challenge (see Chapter 8) and took class wins on the RAC rally.

GT and XS

The 205 GT, one of seven models available from the car's launch in 1983, was somewhat ambitiously called a GT, but it was the top-of-the-range model at the time, with a 1,360cc engine producing 80bhp at 5,800rpm, and it had two single-choke carburettors. Torque was respectable at 81lb.ft and top speed was a healthy 106mph, with acceleration from 0-60mph in 11 seconds. Fuel consumption was 30.7mpg for urban driving, 54.3mpg at a constant 56mph and 40.4mpg at a constant 75 mph. This model, available in five-door form only, was by no means sporty inside, with ribbed velour trim on standard seats, but

This black 205 GTI 1.6 from September 1990 shows the new-style front and rear light lenses and is typical of the many 205 GTIs seen on the roads today.

A stunning example of the GTI 1.9. This particular car won the *Concours d'Elegance* overall at the Peugeot Sport Club's National Convention on three separate occasions. The wheelarches are probably cleaner than when they left the factory.

The 1992 205 Rallye limited edition was available in either yellow or white and was the last car produced to feature the Peugeot Talbot stripes in these colours. The price of this model when new was £7,995.

The interior of the British-specification 205 Rallye limited edition introduced in 1992 was spartan, but it had the same style of seats as the GTI.

The engine bay of the XS (and mechanically identical GT) is less cluttered than that of a GTI.

The interior of an XS is similar to the 1.6 GTI but the Stratos tweed has stripes in the opposite direction and the instrumentation is not so comprehensive.

it did have a rev-counter and a radio/cassette player. Externally, pretty steel wheels (with 165/70SR-13 tyres) were standard, but alloy wheels were an extra cost option. Its only sporting clues were a GT transfer badge stuck on each front wing and a small rear tailgate spoiler. Apart from alloy wheels, the combined option of central locking and electric front windows could be specified as well as the sliding sunroof seen on the GTI. At the end of 1984, the price new was £5,895.

In 1986, a three-door version of the GT was introduced, the XT. This was similar in all respects, but was soon dropped in favour of the XS, a new model which was much closer in specification to the GTI, and competitively priced at £6,845. Insurance for this model was in a very reasonable group 8 versus the GTI's groups 12 and 14. Engine power was increased to 85bhp at 6,400rpm via a twin-choke carburettor, and top speed was now up to 110mph, with a 0-62mph acceleration time of 10.6 seconds. In spite of the increased power, economy on the urban cycle improved to 32.8mpg.

Just 1,200 examples of the Limited Edition were produced at the beginning of 1990. This car is the Miami Blue 1.9 version, sporting extra standard equipment including, for the first time on a 205, power-assisted steering.

A 1989 205 CTI in Metallic Haze Blue. A true four-seater, the 205 Convertible brought practical open-top motoring to many owners.

For the 1988 model year, the GT was renamed the SR and, though it continued with the same engine, all sporting hints were dropped in favour of a more luxurious image. The XS was clearly the sporting model below the GTI and it took the GTI's front spoiler and two long-range driving lamps and sports seats (trimmed in Stratos tweed). Its door panels were trimmed up to window level and carried a red stripe.

In October 1989, the success of the XS prompted Peugeot to re-introduce the GT as a five-door version (including the front spoiler with twin long-range driving lamps) and to delete the SR. The XS was good value at £8,135 and the GT cost £250 more, compared with a 1.6 GTI at £9,835. At this point, central locking became standard on both models. The original alloy wheel option continued right through until the models' deletion in 1992.

In September 1990, the darker grey plastic trim, clear front indicator lenses and redesigned rear light lenses were introduced throughout the 205 range, but there were no further specification changes until the 1992 model year,

which coincided with the introduction of the 106 models, which ultimately would replace much of the 205 range. The XS designation reverted to XT, but the car was otherwise identical. These models were also available with a catalysed 75bhp 1,360cc engine, which yielded a lower top speed of 106mph and 0-62mph acceleration in 11.4 seconds; fuel consumption was 4mpg worse at a constant 56mph, but 2mpg better on the urban cycle. From 1993, because of EEC legislation, only the catalysed model remained available, but in any case the bulk of the 205 range had been phased out by October.

205 turbo diesels
The decision to include a diesel-powered derivative in a book aimed at sporting models may seem a little odd, but anybody who has sampled a car powered by the Peugeot turbo diesel engine would fully justify it. The first model was a Peugeot 405 in 1988, but a 78bhp 1,769cc turbo diesel appeared in the 205 body in September 1990, badged as D Turbo, the 'D' being coloured red, hinting that this

model had sporting intentions. With a 0-62mph time of 12.2 seconds and a top speed of 109mph it was not slow. The in-gear acceleration times were more impressive still, with the 40-70mph increment in fifth gear not much slower than a 1.6 GTI. Most importantly, its fuel economy was impressive, although some way short of the normally-aspirated Peugeot diesels. At a constant 56mph, no less than 61.4mpg was obtainable, with 40.9mpg at a constant 75mph and 42.8mpg on the simulated urban cycle.

The specification was similar to that of the XS and GT models, with the GTI's driving lamps, tinted glass, central locking, four-speaker stereo radio/cassette and rev-counter, along with the stylish steel wheels from the GT. The seats were lifted straight from the GTI, but trimmed in a high-quality Richmond velour. Options were the same as for the XS and GT: alloy wheels, electric front windows, sliding sunroof and power-assisted steering – a useful feature on this model, which was the heaviest of all the 205s apart from the convertibles.

These attractive 13-inch steel wheels are found on the GT, XS and D Turbo models unless the car was fitted with the optional alloy wheels.

A look under the bonnet of a 205 D Turbo.

The 205 T16 won both the 1985 and 1986 World Rally Championships. An example is seen here taking off on one of the many jumps on the 1000 Lakes rally in 1985. *Photo: CTP.*

This immaculate 205 T16 is probably the finest in existence in the UK. In the background is one of its Group B rallying rivals of the mid-Eighties: the Ford RS200.

The 205 D Turbo appeared identical to the 1.4 GT model (except for the absence of badging on the wings), but was powered by a 1,769cc turbodiesel engine.

When launched, the model was by no means cheap at £9,995 (around £400 more than the equivalent petrol-engined model, the GT), but for the 1992 model year a cheaper three-door model was introduced. To compensate owners, these models have enjoyed particularly high residual values. Also available on 1992 models was the option of anti-lock braking. In 1992, to make this engine available at a lower price point, a five-door GRDT was introduced to supplement the range.

During 1993, the 205 range was rationalized as the 106 range was expanded. Many of the lower-specification 205 models were deleted, but with the absence of a 106 turbo diesel, the 205 turbo diesel was available as the Sceptre (which was broadly equivalent to the GRDT model it had replaced) and the STDT. The Sceptre (an old name from the Humber archives) featured power-assisted steering, ventilated front brake discs, 'Plip' remote-control central locking, tinted glass, a sliding glass sunroof and Richmond velour, while the STDT displayed luxury not seen since the limited-edition Gentry automatic model in 1992. It sported the bumpers and side body mouldings from the GTI models, with bright inserts, and 14in alloy wheels that were originally used on the Peugeot 405 GTX. The front spoiler, incorporating driving lamps from the GTI, completed the external styling and, in common with all 1994 models of the 205, there was no grey plastic tailgate trim; badges were applied directly to the painted lower section of the tailgate. Internally, the GTI-style seats were trimmed in Feriane velour, and there was all the equipment of the Sceptre plus a digital clock, electric front windows, optional ABS and the full instrumentation from the GTI.

For 1996, the 205 range was rationalized still further and thereafter was available only with a 1,124cc petrol engine, a 1,580cc petrol engine coupled to automatic transmission, or a 1,769cc normally aspirated diesel.

205 Rallye special edition
Peugeot certainly launched its fair share of special editions in the 205 range. One of these is the 205 Rallye of 1992, which should not be confused with the 'real' 205 Rallye

This is a 'real' 205 Rallye, complete with 103bhp 1,294cc engine. This owner has added long-range driving lamps, additional striping and decals.

The rear of the 205 Rallye had no grey tailgate panel and was painted in body colour. The four colours of the Peugeot Talbot Sport striping had particular significance: red was for sport, blue and yellow were Peugeot's colours and the sky blue was Talbot's colours.

which was only available in left-hand-drive form and not at all in the UK. The main reason for its inclusion in this book is to show the major differences between the two Rallye models. This one had something of a sporting pretence, but when drawing the line as to what really constitutes a 'sporting' 205, this model is the least powerful of those included in this book.

1992 was a very important year for the 205 as the range was being gradually phased out following the October 1991 launch of the 106. The model programme also had to take into account the imminent introduction of the 306 range, which was scheduled for March 1993. Technically, the requirement to sell only catalyst-equipped cars from January 1993 had also forced the hand of manufacturers to re-align their ranges. Lastly, the insurance market had savaged sales of hot hatches, including the 205 GTI, colossal premiums having put the car beyond the reach of many people under 30 years old. Peugeot already had the XS in the range, which was regarded as a 'warm' hatch, so this Rallye model was being offered, albeit only as a limited

Dimma made in excess of 300 kits like this for the 205. Customers could choose from a very wide variety of colours, including bright pink!

This brace of Gutmann 205s have nearly 400bhp between them. The car on the left is equipped with a modified 16-valve engine transplanted from the Peugeot 405 Mi16, further enhanced by twin carburettors and producing nearly 210bhp. The Sorrento Green model sports the Gutmann 'Race Look 2' body kit and is powered by a 16-valve engine producing around 185bhp.

205 Rallye again: Note the colour-coded bumpers, badging and unique 'squared-off' wheelarch trims.

edition, as what might be termed a lukewarm hatch!

The 205 Rallye referred to here can be recognized by its bright white or very bright yellow paintwork! A base model of the 205, the Junior, was also given the yellow paint treatment. The Rallye was based on a lower-specification model with a few well-chosen extras added. The steel wheels and the valances were painted in body colour, but were the same as those of the XL and XR, rather than the type supplied with the XS or GTI. The Peugeot Talbot Sport striping was used boldly on the tailgate, front grille and both rear quarter panels, with the model's name appearing in similar graphics on the tailgate. The PTS stripes had evolved from the red, yellow and dark blue of Peugeot, added to the sky blue colour of Talbot, which by now was a name of the past. Talbot cars had disappeared in 1986 and the Talbot Express van had been facelifted when receiving its Peugeot lion. For 1993, the sky blue had been replaced in the logo with grey, which appeared on the first production model, the 106 Rallye, in October of that year.

The inside of the 205 Rallye was fairly spartan. The door trims, which had red inserts like the GTI, did not reach the bottom of the window and the painted metal stood out like a sore thumb as it was coloured either yellow or white. The carpets were black, as was the entire interior, and there was no centre console.

The seats were the sports type that originated from the GTI, but they were trimmed all over in plain black velour. It was the same material as had been used on the sides of the original 1.6 GTI, but this time the entire seat was covered with the material, relieved only by a miniature Peugeot Talbot Sport logo on the seat, just below the head restraint. This logo also appeared in the centre of the three-spoke steering wheel. The wheel was of the same design as the post-1988 GTI, but it had a plastic in place of the leather rim. Peugeot had always produced two designs of instrument binnacle: GTI and non-GTI. The non-GTI version, which this model featured, had a strip of warning lights in a moulding within the binnacle, with the speedometer located dead centre and a small rev-counter to the left of it.

The biggest difference was seen under the bonnet, where a 1,360cc single-point fuel-injected engine, producing 75bhp, was matched to a five-speed gearbox. Quite a contrast to the 103bhp of the twin-carburettor 1,294cc engine in the 'real' Rallye.

CHAPTER 5

205 GTI special editions

Adding exclusivity to substance

1989 was an excellent year for the 205 GTI. Sales were ever-increasing and the press were still raving about the car, even the 1.6 version. In October 1989, at the Motorfair at Earls Court, Peugeot announced a special edition with a run of only 1,200 cars. This marked the first addition to the 205's colour range since 1984, and the Miami Blue and pearlescent Sorrento Green models at the show both went down well. Half of the production run would be in each colour and an equal number of cars would be produced in each engine size.

The Miami Blue models went on sale first in 1990, and were followed by the Sorrento Green cars a few months later. Most were registered on a G-plate, but a few were held back until August 1, when the H-plate took over. Although they were priced at only about £400 more than their equivalent mainstream models, the improvement in specification provided was worth much more. The 1.6 version had electric windows as standard to complement its now standard central locking. The sliding glass sunroof was also made standard and power-assisted steering, which was a new option for the 205 range, was also listed as part of this model's standard equipment.

The interior featured seats fully upholstered in grey leather, with matching grey carpets and carpet mats. A Clarion four-speaker stereo radio/cassette was also standard, and in fact there were no options listed for this model, the rarity and luxury of which has since been reflected in used prices, which command up to 20 per cent more than for a regular model. These days the interiors from insurance write-offs are widely sought after for fitment to standard cars.

Griffe

At the Paris Salon in late 1990, Peugeot unveiled a specially trimmed version of the 205 GTI 1.9 called the Griffe, which unfortunately never came to the UK, with the exception of maybe one or two cars, one of which, for sure, was used as a demonstration vehicle by Clarion, Peugeot's audio equipment supplier.

Its Laser Green body and matching badging were highlighted by the dark grey anodized alloy wheels that appeared later on the Radio 1 FM model. The bumper inserts would have been too bright if left as red, so these were changed to a mid-grey. Internally, the major change was the standard fitment of full black leather seats and black carpets. Incidentally, Griffe is the French word for claw, thereby providing a link with Peugeot's lion motif.

Gentry

In early 1992, the 205 Gentry was launched as a special edition, again with only a few hundred produced, and coinciding with the launch of the 309 GTI Goodwood special edition. The Gentry was equipped with the (HP14) four-speed automatic transmission, which was mated to the 105bhp 1.9-litre catalysed XU9J1/Z engine. The peak power was produced at 6,000rpm and top speed was nearly

The 205 GTI Griffe was a limited edition for the French market only, painted in Laser Green and having a black full-leather interior.

This 205 Griffe, thought to be the only one in the UK, features grey anodized alloy wheels.

114mph, with a 0-62mph acceleration time of 11.8 seconds. Fuel consumption was 25.9mpg for urban driving, 44.1mpg at a constant 56mph and 33.2mpg at a constant 75mph.

Externally, the Gentry could be identified by the 14-inch alloy wheels that first appeared on the Peugeot 405 GTX back in 1988, as well as chrome bumper and trim inserts and 'Gentry' badging on the tailgate, which lacked the usual grey-painted panel. The paintwork was in either pearlescent Sorrento Green or Aztec Gold metallic.

The interior was arguably the most luxurious ever seen in a 205; in addition to full leather seats (in either tan or black, depending on the paint colour) and a leather-trimmed steering wheel, it had polished wood door inserts, velour carpet mats and electrically heated door mirrors. Equipment derived from the GTI 1.9 included electric front windows, remote-control central locking and power-assisted steering, all of which were standard. A sliding sunroof was an optional extra, and the original price was £12,836. This model's rarity

The 205 Gentry was a limited-edition model with a detuned GTI 1.9 engine mated to a four-speed automatic transmission. The emphasis was on luxury and the car was available finished in either Sorrento Green or Aztec Gold.

The rarest 205 has always been the 'Radio 1 FM' model. Just 25 were produced for the UK market to commemorate 25 years of Radio 1 broadcasting.

The registration number gives this car away. It has been converted to be powered by a Ford Cosworth engine with four-wheel drive.

value (just over 400 of them were sold in the United Kingdom) ensures for it a continuing healthy price on the secondhand market.

GTI Automatic

During 1992, a cancelled order from Japan meant that the United Kingdom received approximately 200 examples of 205 (and 309) GTIs that had been fitted with a four-speed automatic transmission (all of them were right-hand-drive models). They were registered as used cars and the specification of the 205s involved a mixture of 1.6 and 1.9 GTI equipment. The engine was the 1,905cc catalysed 105bhp unit from the 1.9 CTI, but the cars had the 14-inch alloy wheels from the 1.6. The interior was all from the 1.6, but it should be noted that these cars had the luxury of air conditioning as standard. In early 1997, secondhand prices were similar to those of the 1.9 GTI.

The interior of the 1990 Limited Edition featured grey full-leather trim on the seats, with matching grey carpet (in place of the usual red) and grey carpet mats.

205 GTI 1 FM

Peugeot have produced many limited editions of the 205, but the rarest of them all was the 205 GTI 1 FM. Back in 1967, when the first record was spun on Radio 1, it was hard to predict how successful the station would become. For its 25th birthday, in 1992, just 25 individually numbered 205 GTIs were produced and were listed at just over £17,000 each. That seemed a high price to pay, but included in the figure was a donation of £5,000 from Peugeot to the Nordoff-Robbins Music Therapy Centre. There was much publicity for the cars on Radio 1 FM as one of them was being offered as a competition prize. Coincidentally, one of the disc jockeys also bought one!

The specification of the car was the highest ever seen in a 205. Externally, the familiar grey panel on the tailgate was absent (like on most 205 models from the 1993 model year), and the wheels were anodized in a dark grey colour, except for the rim edge. These wheels had been seen previously on the Goodwood special edition 309 GTI model, as well as on the Griffe. Special badging featured on the tailgate, below the side moulding on the front doors, and by the side repeater indicators. The body colour was black.

Internally, the carpet was grey (again a change for all 1993 model year GTIs), but it also came as standard with luxury carpet mats. The seats were fully trimmed in black leather, which had been an option on the French market for some time, and air conditioning was standard, this again being an option in France.

This Dimma model has been further enhanced by the fitment of a 16-valve 160bhp Mi16 engine, a twin-headlamp conversion and a retrimmed tan leather interior.

A 'standard' Dimma, if there is such a thing. Bonnet vents have been fitted to aid cooling of the turbocharged engine.

From the rear, the wide body kit, large rear roof spoiler, performance exhaust and tailgate trim have all been designed to replicate the original Turbo 16.

Power-assisted steering and anti-lock brakes were also standard, as was a sliding glass sunroof – one of the items of equipment that Peugeot otherwise never made standard.

Under the bonnet, where an immobilizer was fitted, this model featured the 122bhp version of the 1.9 engine, including a catalytic converter. The link with music was further enhanced by the standard Clarion sound system. A remote-control compact disc deck with a boot-mounted six-disc CD autochanger could be heard through front-mounted 60-watt Multi-axial three-way speakers and 100-watt Multi-axial two-way speakers

mounted in an acoustic rear parcel shelf. An example was still retailing in excess of £10,000 in 1997.

Variations on a theme

There were two aftermarket conversions to the 205 that warrant special mention as separate models because of the relative volume produced. These are the Dimma wide-body conversion and the Turbo Technics turbocharged version, both of which sold in their hundreds, particularly between 1988 and 1991. Some customers even specified both conversions, as they were complementary.

Dimma wide-body kit

Although there have been many imitations of the 205 GTI during the Nineties, there is only one manufacturer of this kit, which was inspired by the original T16 model and was even approved by Peugeot themselves. The Dimma kit comprised rear wings, which were fitted over the existing body, plus side skirts, front spoiler, rear valance, rear spoiler and replacement front wings. All this could take some 160 hours of labour to fit, and the kit could be specified with 16in split-rim alloy wheels and matching 205/45-16 tyres; these wheels were 7.5x16 at the front and 8x16 at the back. The package cost £5,000 plus VAT. Several other options were available, including leather retrims, bonnet vents, lowered suspension and unique paint options.

Turbo Technics 205

In 1989, for a cost of around £2,500, a 115bhp 1.6 GTI could become a 160bhp machine and the 130bhp 1.9 would

The Dimma stable has also produced a kit for the 309 (in the background) but the 205 Dimma with Peugeot Talbot Sport striping looks the more purposeful.

increase its output to 175bhp with the addition of the Turbo Technics/Garrett T25 turbocharger. Torque figures were even more impressive: 162lb.ft at 3,000rpm and 182lb.ft at 3,000rpm, respectively.

Quoted performance for the 'TT 1.9' was 0-60mph in 6.3 seconds (usually 7.8 seconds), with a top speed of 132mph. 0-100mph could be achieved in just 18 seconds and 50-70mph in a stunningly quick 5 seconds. Another feature on

the 1.9 version was a two-stage boost. A small switch on the dashboard could be operated to provide either medium or high boost (0.65bar).

Many other engine components were uprated, including a larger oil cooler, a front-mounted intercooler and an additional injector mounted in the throttle body. The 1.9 version featured an uprated clutch and a larger exhaust system.

The 205 Turbo Technics conversion was very popular as it had 175bhp available via a two-stage boost system. Visually, the only clues are the wing and tailgate badging and the modified front spoiler for the larger oil cooler.

CHAPTER 6

205 Cabriolets

Two cars in one

Although the 205 GTI was one of only a small number of performance cars Peugeot had manufactured until more recently, there had been no shortage of open-topped models. One can look back to the 302 Roadster or the 403 Cabriolet or, more recently, the Cabriolet versions of the 204, 304 and 504. Indeed, Peugeot went to the trouble of ordering a completely restyled body for the 504 Cabriolet (and Coupe).

But the last of these had been made in the late Seventies, and it was not until 1982 that the company once again listed a Cabriolet model. Furthermore, this was not really a Peugeot at all, but an open-top Talbot Samba, although this in turn was a car which had originally been derived from the Peugeot 104. Both design and manufacture – in limited numbers – of the Cabriolet were entrusted to Pininfarina, in Turin, whose links with Peugeot extended back to the mid-Fifties.

The shape of the 205 was ideally suited to a Cabriolet derivative, and so the car's product planners ensured that when production of the Samba ceased in 1986 an open-top 205 was ready and waiting to take its place on the production lines at Pininfarina's Grugliasco plant. The timing would give the car a very high profile because it meant that it would be produced alongside such Italian classics as the original Alfa Romeo Spider and the Ferrari Testarossa.

Although the 205 saloons were designed and styled in-house by Peugeot, responsibility for the Cabriolet was totally Pininfarina's. The company began with a blank sheet

of paper in May 1983 and had the first part-finished cars rolling off the production line by September 1985. Body parts which were common to all 205 three-door models, such as the bonnet, were shipped from the Mulhouse and Sochaux factories to Italy, where they would be painted and assembled with the unique Cabriolet parts, including the hood, before being sent back to France for final assembly.

Designing an open-top car from a saloon or hatchback presents many problems. Taking the roof away leaves a bodyshell that requires much stiffening, and hence extra weight, so it must be designed thoughtfully to maximize rigidity but at the same time keep the additional weight to a minimum. Under the skin of the 205 are two additional crossmembers, one of which is there to support the rollover hoop. The size of this crossmember can be seen by the intrusion of the carpet where the front seatbelt spools are located. The side sills are also much fatter, and protrude outside the car by around half an inch, although in a manner which is totally in keeping with the style of the body. On the inside they protrude even more, hence the reason for a different carpet pattern for this model. A vinyl pad is provided near the accelerator pedal to stop shoes scuffing the carpet, as it is much closer at this point.

Attention to detail in designing the Cabriolet was very good. For example, the jacking points were strengthened to support the extra weight and consequently a much stronger jack was supplied with the car. Although this is still located beyond the right headlight, a different bracket is welded to the body on which to mount it. Extra metal can also be

When the hood is closed, the CTI displays the same attributes as the 1.6 GTI, although it is 188lb heavier.

found in the windscreen frame, and the doors have been totally redesigned to allow a quarter-light, which again helps rigidity, especially as the doors are frameless.

All this extra metal added around 90lb to the weight of the bare bodyshell, but by the time the car was ready for the road, the weight increase over an equivalent three-door hatchback was approximately 188lb. Most of this was accounted for by the hood mechanism. In terms of performance, it was equivalent to a 1.6 GTI having to carry a 13-stone person in the car all the time. Other points to note were a specially designed centre console that had a larger storage/cassette box and tiny heater ducts for rear seat passengers. Other parts, like the bootlid and rear quarter-panels, were made specially, but much of the work by Pininfarina was on the hood design.

The first two decisions when designing any convertible are how to fold the hood and whether to fit a glass or plastic rear window. A glass window, of course, will not fold and therefore must be much smaller, but it does allow the fitment of a heater element. The 205's rivals, the Golf,

Escort and Astra/Kadett, all had glass windows, but BMW and Mercedes had opted for plastic for their more expensive convertibles. Although this was not as secure as glass, unfortunately any would-be thief would have little trouble breaking into any soft-top car through the fabric of the hood.

The cleverness of the 205 Cabriolet's hood design is that it manages to sit lower than hoods on the Golf and Escort and also impinges less on rear-seat accommodation and boot space. The height of the boot is reduced slightly, in line with the smaller opening, but both width and depth are identical to the hatchback's. The clever design of the rear suspension and the facility of a 50:50 split folding rear seat make the Cabriolet as practical as one could expect. Rear seat width is just a fraction less than in the hatchback. The Cabriolet offers an advantage over other 205s for rear-seat passengers in that they are provided with wind-down windows, if only for two-thirds of the way.

The additional weight of the conversion and the different behaviour of the body meant that changes in the suspension

The hood can be opened or closed in a matter of seconds by one person. A strong catch at the top corner of each windscreen post secures it firmly, but care should be taken not to trap the radio aerial when closing the hood.

With the hood down and the heater on, the four-seater Convertible can be enjoyed, even in the British climate.

This 205 CTI has had its bumpers, trim and tailgate panel colour-coded. Note the snug fit of the hood cover and its relatively low profile compared with other cars in its class.

settings were necessary. Those for the GTI, and its ride height, had already caused complaints at this model's launch in 1984, and as the Cabriolet bodyshell was only likely to make matters worse the decision was taken to use the standard 205's suspension and ride height. It was softer, but with the Cabriolet's lower centre of gravity the handling was still superb and the ride was fully acceptable.

Although production had started in September 1985, the decision had been taken to launch the Cabriolet models at the same time as the revised 205 GTI 1.6 in May 1986. Therefore, all CTI versions had the more powerful 1,580cc engine, producing 115bhp, to help overcome the extra weight penalty. The CTI was the only Cabriolet model available in the UK at the time of the launch, but French customers could opt for the CT, with the 1,360cc 80bhp carburettor-fed engine from the GT.

The GT and CT were related in the same way as the GTI (1.6) and the CTI, although it is interesting to note that a new colour was available at the launch of the CTI that was never to be available on the GTI models. In addition to

white, red, Silver and Graphite Grey, Haze Blue could be specified, a light blue metallic. This is not to be confused with the Topaz Blue that was later found on other Peugeot models, including the 205 GTI for a short time in 1990, although the two colours are very similar.

1986 was the year in which the British public really got to know about the 205 GTI. Insurance premiums had not yet gone through the roof, and owners of early 105bhp 1.6 models were trading them in for the newly-uprated 115bhp engine. This popularity caused supply problems for the CTI, and a delivery time of up to six months prevailed for a while.

1987 saw absolutely no change to the specification but, in line with the 205's major revision in January 1988, the CTI followed suit in nearly all areas. The biggest change was to the dashboard, but the seats remained trimmed in Biarritz velour when the 205 GTI 1.6 changed to the Monaco tweed for 1988 and 1989. The door trims also retained the old style, which did not reach the window sill, but the red fabric pinstripe from the GTI's door trim was adopted.

To aid rigidity, the doors of a 205 Convertible have a fixed quarter-light. Although the trim was modified at the time of the 1988 facelift, Convertible models have never had door trim that reached the window sill.

A revision of colour options occurred in 1989, with the deletion of Haze Blue and changes in the shade of the white and red. The CTI was therefore available in Ivory White, Scarlet Red, Silver and Graphite Grey.

In 1990, following further changes to the 205 specification, an electric hood could be specified as an option, and would become part of the car's standard equipment in August that year. However, this mechanism was hardly the work of art that is offered on the 306 Cabriolet. To operate it on the 205 the clips had first to be released by hand at the top of the windscreen frame, then, with the engine turned off, a button pressed to start six motors and begin pulling at the hood mechanism. After about 15 seconds the operation was complete and the tonneau cover could be fitted if necessary. A similar

procedure had to be repeated in reverse to close the hood.

There was another choice of specification in 1990: the combined option of central locking, front electric windows and metallic paint. Atlantic Blue metallic also became available as an option. The combined option remained with the CTI right through to the end of production, even though central locking became part of the GTI 1.6's standard equipment from August 1989, although the change to the BE-3 gearbox was made to both the GTI and the CTI at the same time. 1990 also brought crystal clear front indicators and new-style rear light lenses, and at this stage the interior came into line with the GTI 1.6 again, with Quartet velour (black and red) adorning the centre seat portions and plain black velour on the remainder of the seat.

Apart from the gearbox, the only change ever made to the

Although the boot is of comparable size to the 205 hatchback's, the opening is much smaller and access a little restricted.

mechanical specification of the CTI took place in late 1991. With the need to produce all cars with a catalytic converter from the beginning of 1993, Peugeot decided not to make a catalysed version of the XU5JA 1,580cc engine which, of course, spelt the end of the GTI 1.6. Peugeot already had the 1,580cc engine in differing states of tune for the 205 (a 90bhp version could be found in the 205 Automatic).

Meanwhile, the 1,905cc engine was available in four different power levels, the lowest being a single-carburettor version producing around 108bhp in the 405 GR. With single-point fuel injection and a catalytic converter fitted, it produced 105bhp. It was this engine, the XU9J1/Z, that appeared in the CTI (the 'Z' in the engine code was an abbreviation for catalyst). Although the maximum power figure was down by 10bhp, the torque output was marginally more at 105lb.ft against 99lb.ft. Both

performance and fuel economy were affected slightly, top speed becoming 115mph (previously 118mph) and fuel consumption on average 3mpg worse.

At this time, the colour choice altered again and Peugeot's own Alpine White and Scarlet Red were used for the vast majority of the final models. Air conditioning also became an option in October 1991. The imminent launch of the 306 Cabriolet was to be the signal to end production of the 205 Cabriolet, and the last cars were registered in the UK in early 1994.

205 CJ

This model was launched in June 1988, when the popularity of open-top motoring was increasing but few cheap cars were available. At a starting price of £8,835 it cost less than anything Ford, Vauxhall or Volkswagen were producing. The origins of this model were in the Junior, which was at

The black hood and dark grey trim make this metallic blue CTI look particularly nice in Nice!

The CT was launched in France at the same time as the CTI, as a predecessor to the mechanically identical CJ. This car does not feature standard wheels; it should have the same steel wheels as on the XS and GT.

The 205 CJ is a very sought-after car, being the UK market's cheapest four-seater convertible for much of its life.

the bottom of the 205 range. The name CJ is an abbreviation of Cabriolet Junior, and the Junior components borrowed included the entire interior, with blue denim cloth seats with contrasting stitching and blue carpets. 'CJ' badging on the front wings and side tapes were prominent. The engine was the single-carburettor version of the 1,360cc TU unit, producing 70bhp. The interior was quite spartan, with basic instrumentation (no rev-counter) and an analogue clock, but a Clarion digital radio/stereo cassette was fitted, with two door-mounted speakers.

Despite the extra weight and with just 70bhp available, performance was most satisfactory, with a top speed of 101mph and a claimed 0-60mph time of around 12.5 seconds. It was very miserly at the pumps, too, 58.9mpg being achieved at a steady 56mph.

Until 1990, all the CJ models seemed to be produced only in Ivory White, but later on two metallic colours, Azur Blue (a turquiose) and Silver Grey, became available. In August 1990, the electrically powered hood from the CTI was available as an option at £525.

In October 1991, the only mechanical change in the life of the CJ took place with the standard fitment of a three-way catalytic converter. As this meant fitting monopoint fuel injection, power was increased to 75bhp and the top speed went up to 106mph, with 0-60mph taking just over 11 seconds. However, fuel economy suffered, with just 48.7mpg at a steady 56mph. The last models, from 1993, were produced in Alpine White or Miami Blue, with a final price of £11,535, and the model was deleted in early 1994, at the same time as the CTI.

205 Roland Garros

Peugeot have produced Roland Garros versions of the 205 hatchback and Cabriolet and subsequently of the 106 and 306. (Roland Garros, after whom the French national tennis stadium was named, was a great French aviator.) Peugeot marketed these models in a dark green metallic, with seats that were half-covered in white leather and with a white matching leather steering wheel. Most distinguishable, though, was the matching white hood that

The limited-edition Roland Garros Convertible is the rarest soft-top; just 150 right-hand-drive models were produced for the UK.

was fitted to the limited run of just 150 right-hand-drive Cabriolet models that were produced in June 1989 with a price of £12,980. They were powered by the 1,360cc 85bhp engine from the XT and GT models and had as standard the alloy wheels that had been available as an option on the GT, XT and XS since 1983. There were 450 hatchback Roland Garros models launched at the same time and both variants are now very much sought after.

205 CTI – driving impressions

My fifth 205 was a 1989 Haze Blue 205 CTI. It was purchased secondhand at the end of the winter, when prices were at their lowest. This, in fact, was my first encounter with the 115bhp engine since that initial test drive in 1987. It certainly countered the additional 188lb weight of the Cabriolet, and acceleration was comparable to that of the 105bhp 1.6 GTIs I had owned before.

With the hood up, and especially at night, you would be hard-pushed to tell the difference from the 'tin top' models. However, traffic noise, especially when overtaking large vehicles, was more pronounced as the hood allowed more noise in. The view from the driver's seat was somewhat interrupted by the additional quarter-light frames and there was a large blind spot to the rear as a result of the heavy C-

pillars. Rain noise was more pronounced, too, but unlike so many open-top cars from the past, the car never leaked. My only criticism was the lack of guttering on the roof, which meant that rain water ran into the car when opening the door.

When it was cold or it had rained, visibility through the plastic rear window was either poor or non-existent as a result of raindrops on the outside and no rear wash/wipe, or condensation on the inside and no heated panel. When the rear window had iced over I found warm water to be the best option as I didn't trust de-icer on the plastic, while an ice scraper would have scratched the plastic permanently. Even a chamois leather would scratch the window if there was dirt on it, but treated with great care it should last around six years. After this, though, it starts to get brittle and can split, and where it folds it will gradually turn opaque; the entire window becomes cloudy with age. Additionally, the two ridges in the tiny parcel shelf leave permanent marks on the plastic when the hood is folded for any length of time.

The best way of preventing this is to leave a large black towel on the shelf permanently. If the window is cracked, or vandalized, a replacement would cost just over £200 in 1997. However, check the small print of your insurance

Neat styling of the basic 205 lent itself well to the Cabriolet derivation, design and manufacture of which were entrusted to Pininfarina, hence the badging. The wind-down rear quarter-light is an eminently practical feature.

While the Cabriolet retains all the mechanical features of the saloon version, modifications to the bodyshell are more extensive than at first meets the eye, as great care has been taken to reinforce the structure in compensation for the absence of a roof panel.

Facia of the Cabriolet follows the saloon pattern, but the doors are unique to the open model as the main windows are frameless and only the quarter-lights have a surround. Wider sills than those of the saloon, part of the bodyshell reinforcement for the Cabriolet, necessitate detail changes to the floor covering.

69

policy; *window* replacement should cover all but the usual £50 excess whereas *glass* replacement will cover nothing. Also, this is not an easy job for the windscreen fitters and it may take a couple of hours to get it to fit perfectly.

The operation of the hood soon became a simple affair and for me the hood cover became redundant; it may have made the car look neater, but it just wasn't worth the trouble. The hood is perfectly safe just resting on the car, even at over 100mph on an *autobahn*. However, care should be taken to ensure that the hood, and particularly the window, folds with the minimum of creasing, as that will show permanently. I found the best method was to undo the clips and walk towards the back of the car holding the hood, rather than pushing from the inside. In reverse, it was easier to stand at the back of the car and push the hood, using one of the hoops inside. The radio aerial was always kept in a near-vertical position to minimize the chances of trapping it when closing the hood.

If it started to rain while I was driving with the hood down (and it did on many occasions in Great Britain) I found that very little rain would penetrate the passenger compartment at motorway speeds and a bridge would usually appear within a short distance. The whole operation took around 10 seconds.

In general, the handling of the car was similar to that of the GTI except that the softness of the front suspension was very noticeable. This was accentuated when stopping at a give-way sign, but the lower centre of gravity meant less body roll. The brakes and tyres were sufficient, but I would have preferred the all-disc set-up of the 1.9 version and its 15-inch rims.

Passengers liked the car as much as I did. With the roof down it was definitely a head-turner, and the raspy exhaust note and wind-in-the-hair feeling was unbeatable. There was not much wind buffeting, thankfully; front-seat passengers would experience little more than a ruffling of the hair at speeds up to 70mph unless they happened to be over 6ft tall. It was much worse, though, with the windows down. Inevitably, rear-seat passengers fared worse, and it would have to be a shorter journey at a modest speed rather than a motorway cruise for them to be comfortable. The standard audio equipment only specified speakers in the front, but conversation was still possible. At night, the roof-down mode was very effective in town, where speed was less important than style, and it was particularly nice to have unlimited supplies of fresh air, not just a stream through a vent.

Of course, using the car when the hood was down meant that a penalty had to be paid at the fuel pumps, consumption typically increasing from 32mpg to just 30mpg over a long journey. The additional weight of the car had already dented the figure, and the 115bhp engine was thirstier than the original unit from 1984. Apart from the hood, most of the parts were the same price as for the GTI, but looking for secondhand parts that were particular to the CTI was a fruitless task. In particular, the gas strut that opens the bootlid is shorter than the tailgate struts of the GTI and, as there is only one, it tends to wear out quickly.

I found that this model's versatility came into its own at the DIY stores, and whereas most people were struggling with awkward and long objects, loading bulky items was simplicity itself with the roof down. Long objects would rest on the top of the windscreen frame, with the other end stuck into the boot via the folding rear seat sections. In my estimation, no other car has been able to match its ability to transport four passengers or large quantities of luggage or purchases, its stylishness and the immense driving pleasure it offers, all at such a reasonable price. Despite the group 13 insurance rating and the inevitable security risks, the cost of ownership was balanced by glacial depreciation. With secondhand prices ranging between £3,000 and £9,000 at 1997 values, it offers so much car for the money and consequently it makes a very sensible buy. I did miss the ultimate speed of the 1.9, though, but of course, there are conversions …

CHAPTER 7

205 Turbo 16

"Sir, we have won"

1981 was a key year for the motorsport activities of Peugeot and Talbot. The Peugeot 504 V6 Coupe was rallying successfully in Africa and the Lotus-powered Talbot Sunbeam was on its way to first place in the World Rally Championship. A young man by the name of Jean Todt, who was a co-driver in a Talbot Sunbeam that year, was also a consultant for Peugeot, and his role became more and more prominent during that year. When poor health dictated the retirement of the head of the competitions department, Gérard Allégret, it soon became clear that there was only one suitable person to lead the department, and Peugeot's President, Jean Boillot, made that appointment on October 19, 1981, giving the post to Todt.

The major project was still being defined, but there was to be a rally version of the M24 (Peugeot's codename for the 205). It was decided at a very early stage that the 205 and its rallying version would appear simultaneously. Jean Boillot realized how important the project was, and Talbot pulled out of Formula One so they could concentrate solely on this project at the Peugeot research and technical centre at La Garenne-Colombes, near Paris. Jean Boillot made regular contact with the committee that had been formed to design the car, and it was he alone who gave the green light each time, and he and Jean Todt christened the car 205 Turbo 16, a name that stood out as there were very few 16-valve turbocharged engines in existence then.

It would compete in the Group B rallying category in which the Audi Quattro was such a dominant force, and ultimately against rival cars such as the Lancia Delta S4,

MG Metro 6R4, Ford RS 200 and Renault 5 Turbo 2. It was to be the first purpose-built rally car, and the design committee had decided upon a four-wheel drive system, with a turbocharged mid-engine of just under 1,800cc, giving an adjusted displacement, after applying the factor for turbocharging, of 2.5 litres.

The XU engine, which was about to be fitted to the Peugeot 305 and Citroen BX, was chosen as the base, and soon the 1,775cc XU8T was born, with a standard output of 200bhp. Had the committee been influenced differently, it might well have been to use a version of the V6 Douvrin engine seen in the Peugeot 604, Renault 30 and Volvo 264.

The requirements for Group B rallying were established, which meant that 200 roadgoing versions of the Turbo 16 had to be produced for homologation purposes. The design was finished and the first prototype was built during 1982. Both interior and exterior styling were completed, along with all the things we take for granted on normal road cars, such as sound-deadening.

February 23, 1983 was the day for the simultaneous launch of the 205 and the Turbo 16, the 205 being displayed at the Geneva motor show while the Turbo 16 appeared in Paris. During the preceding weeks, 5,000 standard 205s had been delivered throughout France to owners who had been given a sneak preview of the new model. By August, the Turbo 16 had reappeared as a Group B prototype that was essentially the Evolution model, with 320bhp, and just two months later the 205

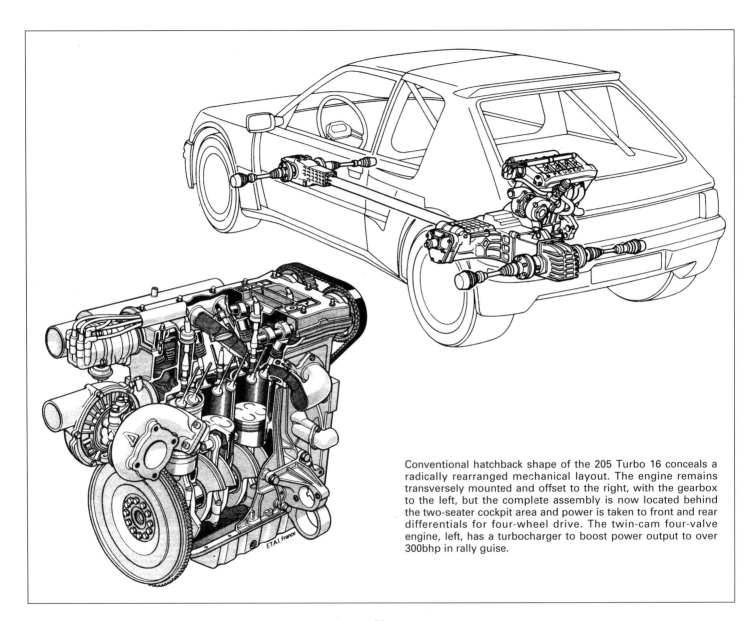

Conventional hatchback shape of the 205 Turbo 16 conceals a radically rearranged mechanical layout. The engine remains transversely mounted and offset to the right, with the gearbox to the left, but the complete assembly is now located behind the two-seater cockpit area and power is taken to front and rear differentials for four-wheel drive. The twin-cam four-valve engine, left, has a turbocharger to boost power output to over 300bhp in rally guise.

Low stance and much-widened wheelarches give the Turbo 16 a very different visual impact from the standard front-engined models, an effect enhanced in the case of this exhibition example by dramatic competition-style graphics.

Suspension of the 205 Turbo 16 is a no-compromise competition-oriented layout, with double wishbones all round and a high degree of adjustability to facilitate tuning the car for specific events.

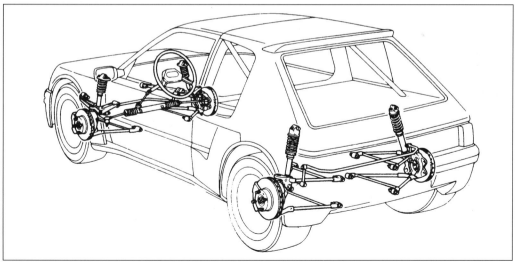

Turbo 16 was driven in public for the first time in the Sarlat rally, although the car's official debut was not to be until the 1984 Corsican rally.

1984

The intention was that 1984 would be primarily a preparation and development year for the team whilst taking part in five World Championship rallies: Corsica, Acropolis, 1000 Lakes, San Remo and the RAC; the team's serious assault on the World Championship would follow in 1985. Two drivers had been approached to drive the Turbo 16: Jean-Pierre Nicolas, who had been the principal test driver, and the Finn, Ari Vatanen, who would drive the No 1 car.

The Corsican rally, in May 1984, was the first real test for the Turbo 16, and from a marketing viewpoint, its timing, coinciding with the launch of the 205 GTI 1.6, was perfect;

a good result would do the Peugeot marque an immense favour. Vatanen, who set a stage record with his new car, held the lead for much of the event, but unfortunately he spun out of contention after hitting a stream of water. However, Nicolas held on to take fourth place, an excellent debut result.

The Acropolis rally, in Greece just over three weeks later, was to prove less successful and both cars were non-finishers. Vatanen had covered 32 out of the 47 stages before he retired due to a broken oil pump drive, and Nicolas fared only a little better, retiring on stage 38 with a broken brake caliper. However, the Peugeot team had learnt a lot on its first gravel rally and many components had proved their reliability, but the need to win an event was increasing.

The team deliberately missed the Argentine and New Zealand rallies in order to spend more time on development

This 205 Turbo 16 was prepared by Des O'Dell's competitions department at the Coventry factory for Mikael Sundstrom.

between the Acropolis and the 1000 Lakes in Finland, scheduled for the end of August. Work was already underway on the Evolution 2 version for 1985, but meanwhile the current car was steadily improved and maximum power went up from 320 to 350bhp. Vatanen took the car to Finland to test the suspension over the famous Finnish jumps, and problems encountered there were only just resolved in time for the rally after help from Bilstein, the shock absorber manufacturer. Newly designed parts arrived on the morning of the rally for the 205, only one car having been entered because, traditionally, non-Scandinavians did not do well on this event.

Responding to the tough opposition from the Audis and Lancias, fine-tuning of the Peugeot continued during the course of the rally, and the Turbo 16 gained on the leading Lancia on stage after stage until Ari Vatanen, with Terry Harryman as his co-driver, took over the lead and kept it to the end. Peugeot had won its first World Championship rally. Jean Todt called the Peugeot President by telephone: "Sir, we have won."

In the San Remo rally, at the end of September, Vatanen found himself in the lead from the outset. He was by far the quickest driver, setting 31 out of 54 fastest stage times, and despite going off on a stage during a thunderstorm, he went on to win the rally from Audi, his 205 suffering only broken driving lamps. Nicolas, meanwhile, struggled with turbocharger problems on what was to be his last rally, but despite this setback he still finished fifth.

The team spent some time testing in Kenya in preparation for 1985, but they still entered one car on the RAC rally. Vatanen took the lead and held it until a driving error on the last day caused him to go off. He managed to retake the lead from the chasing Hannu Mikkola in the Audi Quattro, but soon after one of the 205's drive-shafts broke. After repairs, the superior stage times of the Turbo 16 enabled Vatanen to regain the lead, and hang on to it, for Peugeot's third victory.

1985
As this was to be the team's serious assault on the WRC, more top-class drivers were needed. Jean Todt had decided to employ three of them: two would drive in all 11 World

One of the most stunning victories of all time was Ari Vatanen's on the 1985 Monte Carlo rally (pictured here). *Photo: CTP.*

Championship rallies, the third would drive on the longer-distance events and act as a test driver in between. Walter Röhrl and Markku Alen both turned down the offer of a drive, opting to stay with Audi and Lancia, respectively. So Vatanen, who was retained, was joined by fellow Finn Timo Salonen and his co-driver Seppo Harjanne. The third driver was to be Frenchman Bruno Saby, partnered by Jean-François Fauchille.

The first round was the Monte Carlo and all three cars were entered. The Turbo 16 trailed the Audi Quattro on the dry stages, but in the snow it soon caught up and Vatanen took over the lead. Although eight minutes of time penalties were incurred when co-driver Harryman checked in four minutes early, Vatanen was able to make up the time deficit on the last stage, thanks to an inspired tyre choice. Salonen was third and Saby fifth.

In Sweden, modifications were made to the car to cope with the cold conditions, and these helped Vatanen to another first place. He had led the rally from stage 2 to the finish, and Salonen came home third. This rally helped Peugeot to put their name firmly on the map in Scandinavia at a time when the success of the 205 range as a whole had given the company a 20 per cent lift in sales.

Whilst preparing for Portugal, the team were also busy developing 20 Evolution 2 models that were due to compete later in the year. This event marked a turning point, for Salonen was now proving to be a fraction quicker than Vatanen on asphalt, and when Vatanen retired with broken suspension Salonen was left with the task of catching the leaders and winning the rally. He did just that.

The Safari rally lasted for five days and covered 3,225 miles, with time controls along the way to establish running and finishing positions. Peugeot entered three cars, all modified heavily to cope with the extreme conditions and length of the rally, but Vatanen suffered a blown head gasket after his radiator had failed and Saby drove too quickly into a wadi and damaged his car beyond repair. Salonen soldiered on to finish seventh, which was a relatively good achievement for a car's first appearance on an event like this.

Corsica was effectively the Turbo 16's first birthday and it was marked with the competition debut of the Evolution 2. The main changes to the car centred around power (now increased to 450bhp), torsional rigidity (45-50 per cent stiffer), lightness and aerodynamics. An Evolution 2 model can be distinguished by the huge black roof spoiler, additional aerodynamic aids at the front, and flat wheel covers.

Peugeot entered three cars for the Corsican rally, only one of which was an Evolution 2 model, which was still in need of further development work. Nevertheless, Bruno Saby managed to take second place with it. Salonen lasted only one stage before retiring with ignition failure, whilst Vatanen crashed out on stage 14 when trying to make up time after two earlier punctures. This was the first time that an Aerospatiale helicopter was used to track the cars on the longer stages and fly in a mechanic if there was a problem. Obviously relationships between Peugeot and Aerospatiale had improved since the episode mentioned in Chapter 2!

The Acropolis rally in Greece saw Peugeot return to winning ways with Salonen leading from start to finish, although Vatanen was less lucky after steering failure caused his retirement on stage 2. By this stage of the World Rally Championship Peugeot were clear leaders with 92 points, the nearest challengers being Audi with 62 points, and there were six other manufacturers with 30 points or less.

So a month later, when the team went down-under for the New Zealand rally, the Championship was clearly an Audi-Peugeot battle. On this event, Audi were to prove quicker on the straight sections, but slower on the twisty bits, and as there were more twisty bits than straights, Peugeot duly took their first double, Salonen leading Vatanen home.

The Argentinian rally will be remembered most for the accident that left Ari Vatanen seriously injured. His car left

The Turbo 16 returns to the 1985 Tour de Corse one year after its maiden victory. Note the increasing importance of aerodynamics, with the larger rear spoiler and modifications to the front with deflectors. *Photo: CTP.*

Mikael Sundstrom in action on the 1986 RSAC Scottish rally with co-driver Voitto Silander.

the road on only the second stage and Ari and co-driver Terry Harryman suffered fractured vertebrae. Vatanen was kept in intensive care and eventually flown back to Finland; at one stage he slipped into a coma, but thankfully he pulled through and eventually made a total recovery, likewise Harryman.

It was thought that one of the idiosyncracies of the car – its tendency to land nose-first after a jump due to the torque of the transversely-mounted engine – might have contributed to the cause. It is also estimated that Vatanen's car had left the road at a speed in excess of 130mph. As for the rally, Peugeot had entered a third car at the last moment, driven by former Argentinian Formula One driver Carlos Reutemann. He came home third after Salonen had scored yet another victory. If it had not been for a privateer taking second place in an Audi, Peugeot would have won the Championship that day.

With Vatanen unable to drive for the remainder of the season, Jean Todt recruited Kalle Grundel, who had been driving a T16 for Peugeot's German subsidiary. The 1000

Lakes rally was the setting for the World Championship victory for which Peugeot were now hot favourites. Salonen completed the job in style, winning all but six of the 50 stages for a fine victory, supported by Grundel in fifth place. This was the first victory for the E2 version, which by this time was producing 430bhp at 7,500rpm and enjoying a weight advantage of 70kg over its nearest competitor.

So Peugeot and Salonen were World Rally Champions, and there were still three rounds to go. It meant that the rallies at San Remo and the Ivory Coast and Britain's Lombard RAC were of somewhat academic interest to Peugeot as regards World Championship points, but an additional second placing was achieved by Timo Salonen at San Remo.

1986

Defending a title is often harder than winning one, but despite stiffer competition in the shape of the Lancia Delta S4 and the Evolution 2 version of the Audi Sport Quattro,

the six victories (taking Peugeot's total of WRC victories to 15) and a further 10 top-five finishes were nothing short of dominance.

Having conceded victory to the late Henri Toivonen at Monte Carlo, Salonen finished second, with new driver Juha Kankkunen and his co-driver Juha Piironen finishing fifth in their first event for Peugeot after moving from Toyota.

Three weeks later, Kankkunen showed his potential with victory in Sweden, and a useful fifth place on the Marlboro Safari rally at the end of March.

Bruno Saby took his only WRC victory with a T16 in the 1986 Tour de Corse, with co-driver Jean-Francois Fauchille, and despite an improving Lancia Delta S4, Kankkunen won consecutively the Acropolis and New Zealand rallies, backed up by Saby's third place in Greece and Salonen's fifth in New Zealand.

Peugeot B555 SRW is now at home in the Museum of British Road Transport in Coventry.

Stig Blomqvist and Bruno Berglund teamed up and took third place in Argentina, which preceded Scandinavian domination on the 1000 Lakes rally in September. Salonen's first place, Kankkunen's second and Blomqvist's fifth secured the Manufacturer's Championship for Peugeot; the only thing still up for debate was which Peugeot driver would take the driver's crown!

Before the Olympus rally in the United States, at the end of the year, where Kankkunen finished second, the Lombard RAC rally provided the setting for the Driver's Championship to be decided. Salonen duly obliged, winning the event and arriving at the finish in Bath to a rapturous welcome. Kankkunen finished third and the British-entered T16 E2, driven by Mikael Sundstrom and co-driver Voitto Silander, took fourth place.

Sadly, though, 1986 would always be remembered for two other incidents which brought Group B rallying to an end. Poor crowd control led to four spectators being killed and scores more injured in the Portuguese rally, and Henri

Toivonen and his co-driver Sergio Cresto were killed when their Lancia Delta S4 left the road in Corsica and literally exploded.

205 Turbo 16 Grand Raid
After Henri Toivonen was killed and Group B cars were banned, Peugeot turned its attention to Africa and the Rallye Raids with a much-modified 205 Turbo 16. This car, and the 405 Turbo 16 which replaced it in 1988, were to win an unprecedented 11 out of 11 events.

1987
The 205 Turbo 16 Grand Raid, over a foot longer due to an extended wheelbase and the insertion of long-range fuel tanks, won the event at the first time of asking. The car, in its bright yellow Camel Racing Services bodywork, was driven and co-piloted by the strong Vatanen-Giroux combination. The 1987 Paris-Algiers-Dakar rally was Vatanen's comeback drive after the horrific accident in

A rare high-angle shot of a 205 Grand Raid at full speed on the 1988 Paris-Dakar rally.

Argentina in 1985, and in winning this 8,000-mile event he proved he was in a class of his own. A second 205 Turbo 16 came in fifth, driven and co-piloted by Shekhar Mehta and Mike Doughty. Later in the year, Vatanen repeated the feat by winning the Pharoahs rally, this time with new co-driver Bruno Berglund. A first attempt at the Pikes Peak rally, in Colorado, using a lightened 205 Turbo 16 Grand Raid, resulted in an impressive second placing.

1988

The 205 Turbo 16 Grand Raid repeated its previous year's performance on the Paris-Dakar rally, but this time with Juha Kankkunen at the wheel. The team's sponsorship had changed and the car sported the white-and-blue Pioneer livery. This car also won the Tunisia rally and the Atlas rally later in the year, driven by Ari Vatanen, before it gave way to the mechanically similar 405 Turbo 16, which won the Pikes Peak event on its debut. A third place on the Baja rally by rallying's leading female driver at the time, Michele Mouton, rounded off a successful year for the Grand Raid. Peugeot had finished 1-2-3 on the Baja, with 405 Turbo 16s filling the first two places.

1989

The mantle of success in long-distance events now fell firmly on the equally purposeful 405 Turbo 16, which took first place in the Paris-Dakar rally. Earlier, the winning car had made the headlines when, despite the tight security

Back in action again. The 205 Grand Raid once more, this time on the 1989 Paris-Dakar rally.

After the demise of Group B rallying and Rallye Raids, this Turbo 16 E2 was seen in rallycross action at Brands Hatch in May 1990, piloted by Terje Schie.

surrounding such an event, it was stolen, although it was subsequently recovered and continued unimpeded to the finish.

After Peugeot won the Pike's Peak event with the 405 Turbo 16, the team's intended last outing before impending regulation changes was to be the 1989 Pharoah's rally. At the finish line, where all three cars crossed in formation, the first two places were filled by the 405s, but third position went to a 205 Turbo 16 driven by Michele Mouton. This was all the more remarkable as this car was designated as the rapid response vehicle and was carrying in excess of 100kg of spare parts for the other two cars!

1990

The promised changes in regulations never materialized and so Peugeot entered the Paris-Dakar rally for the last time in

1990. A 1-2-3 finish was accomplished with two 405s, along with a 205 Turbo 16, driven by Alain Ambrosino and co-piloted by Alain Baumgartner, which came in third. An historic finish eluded Peugeot when a second 205 Turbo 16, driven by Philippe Wambergue, suffered from clutch problems.

The road version

Regulations dictated that for homologation purposes all Group B rally cars had to be based on a roadgoing model of which at least 200 had been made, hence the 200 'standard' T16s that were produced for sale in 1984. Many of these were subsequently adapted for rallying, rallycross or in some cases written-off, and it is estimated that only about 30 of these standard cars are left in the world and only one or two of them in Great Britain, despite the fact that additional

The Turbo 16 looked particularly aggressive from the front. No kit could ever fully replicate the style of this car, especially the bonnet vent.

The interior of the Turbo 16 owes much to the GTI, but with the instruments housed in this binnacle, which fits over the normal facia. Note the aluminium pedals.

models produced during the car's short life took the final production total to 241.

This model was designed before the GTI and therefore gave its overall style to its humbler brother, not the other way round, and explains similarities such as the interior trim, Speedline alloy wheels and red bumper and trim inserts. It was purely coincidental that the light grey/dark grey seat trim, identical to the trim that appeared in the 1.9

GTI in late 1986, was known as Quattro. Note: the car pictured above has been retrimmed in full grey leather.

The bonnet of the T16 lifts at the front to reveal just the spare wheel, while the entire rear section of the car can be lifted and supported on two struts to allow access to the engine. There is a small carpeted parcel shelf just behind the inner glass window behind the driver.

Physically, there is little in common between the T16

Lifting the rear hatch on this Turbo 16 is a two-man job to reveal the pristine XU8T engine just as it left the assembly line.

Under the bonnet is a spare wheel and the fuel cap, giving other motorists an interesting sight when refuelling.

The rear of a roadgoing Turbo 16. There are reputed to be less than 30 remaining in the world today.

and GTI models, although part of the roof, the doors and mirrors, grille, headlights and driving lamps, and front and rear indicator lenses, are identical, and on the inside, the facia is also similar, although on the Turbo 16 it is hidden behind a full-width instrument panel, which is unique to this model and carries a row of gauges in the centre to supplement the dials in front of the driver. All 200 of the 'homologation' run were made in left-hand drive, and went on sale in France for 290,000FF (approximately £36,000) in 1984.

CHAPTER 8

The 205 in motorsport

Rallies, races and raids

Despite the 205's new-found status as 'performance car of the decade', it would never make a big impact on the racing circuits in the United Kingdom. However, it did appear, in small numbers in the hands of private entrants, in various saloon car championships and in particular the Slick 50 Road Saloon Championship, but essentially, the history of Peugeot's motorsport background in the the UK lies with rallying.

The involvement of a version of the 205 in rallying began in 1984 with the T16, as already covered in more detail in Chapter 7. But it was in 1988 that Des O'Dell, former Director of Motorsport at Peugeot, initiated a scheme to select and develop what was to become the nucleus of Britain's future rallying talent.

After the demise of the T16 at the end of 1986, Peugeot's UK rallying activities were spearheaded over the next two years by the appearance of Group A 205 GTIs in the Shell Oils RAC Open Rally Championship, with drivers who included Terry Kaby and Louise Aitken-Walker, who went on to become rallying's first Ladies World Champion.

Louise campaigned a Group A 205 GTI 1.6 with co-driver Ellen Morgan and took a very impressive class win in 1987 with a clean sweep of five victories, which also included seventh place overall on the Circuit of Ireland rally and sixth overall on the National Breakdown rally, beating many more powerful cars in the process and earning her the prestigious title of *Autosport* National Rally Driver of the Year. The car was prepared jointly by Peugeot Talbot Sport, in Coventry, and Chartersport, based near Aldershot,

who were leading players in Peugeot rallying until the operation closed at the beginning of the Nineties.

In March 1988, Peugeot announced the beginning of the GTI Rally Club, with three preselected drivers – Warren Hunt, Iwan Roberts and a 19-year-old Colin McRae – acting as guinea-pigs for an enlarged series in 1989. The purpose of the Club was to form a championship that would nurture and help develop the talent of Britain's brightest young rally drivers.

So the GTI Rally Challenge was born, and although Colin McRae, Britain's hottest property amongst rally drivers, had departed to drive for Ford, a group of 30 205 and 309 GTIs started the eight-round series, the prize at the end of the contest being a works-supported drive on the Lombard RAC rally. Paul Frankland and co-driver Keith Chipchase won the series and so became the pairing to drive the works-assisted 309 GTI on the RAC rally at the end of the season. This was followed in 1990 with the award of a works drive in a Group A 205 GTI 1.6 in the Shell Oils British Open Rally Championship.

1990 heralded the beginning of a new era for British rallying as one of the UK's top stars, Richard Burns, completed his first full season of rallying in a 205 GTI 1.9. Then a fresh-faced 19-year-old from near Reading, he dominated the season and would have sewn up the GTI Cup sooner had it not been for an infringement at a control point early in the season. His prize was again a works drive on the Lombard RAC rally. Almost 100 competitors took part, divided into two main classes: the Super Cup was

The 205 GTI proved to be a real success as part of the Peugeot Rally Club's package for Britain's future rallying stars. The camaraderie between the crews at events was unrivalled.

Richard Burns (pictured as a Peugeot GTI Rally Challenge driver in 1991) is unquestionably the success story of the Peugeot Rally Club. Starting with the Rally Challenge in 1990, he went on to become England's No 1 rally driver.

aimed at previous competitors, while the GTI Challenge was directed at newcomers and juniors, who were rallying the two versions of the 205 GTI and the 309 GTI. Competitors could enter six rallies, as well as a rallycross event at Croft and a race meeting at Donington Park. Generous prize and bonus money were hallmarks of the Challenge, amounting to over £135,000 in 1990, which encouraged so many competitors to make that important

step onto the first rung of British rallying's ladder at the wheel of relatively inexpensive yet competitive car.

Over the following two years the competition built on the success of the first two, led by Challenge co-ordinator Keith Baud. Entries reached a record level of over 100 in 1991, topped by the reigning Champion, Richard Burns. Richard teamed up for the first time with co-driver Robert Reid, and they opened up an unassailable lead by winning the first

Johnny Milner heads the field with his 205 rallycross car at Brands Hatch in 1989.

three events. By August, the GTI Challenge Cup had been won again by Burns after his seventh victory of the season, on the Kayel Graphics rally.

Elsewhere in the Peugeot rallying world, Johnny Milner, in the works Group A 205 GTI 1.9, came home third overall in a round of the Mintex National Rally Championship ahead of much more powerful machinery. In the Shell Oils Open Rally Championship, Hakan Eriksson (younger brother of Kenneth) and Paul Frankland successfully campaigned the new 210bhp Group A 309 GTI 16 to class victories.

In 1992, to make the car more competitive on National and International rallies, the specification, which had previously been based on Group N rules, was upgraded to 'Challenge' level, which included a limited-slip differential, better braking and the option to remove items of trim. At the end of the season, Brendan Crealey emerged the overall winner and the lucky driver of the works-supported drive on the RAC rally. He went on to further success with another manufacturer in the following season. There was success,

too, at the end of the season for Johnny Milner, whose 1,600cc 205 GTI enabled him to win the Lombard Junior British Rally Championship. The peak entry level of 58 Peugeots (mostly 205 GTIs) was reached on the Zwick Stages rally in Ludlow in September that year.

With the introduction of performance models within the smaller 106 range, the emphasis began to swing away from the 205 GTI as a rally car, and the efforts of the Peugeot Talbot Sport team were concentrated increasingly on their Peugeot 405 entry in the British Touring Car Championship race series.

1993 was the last year for the 205 as a staple rally car, eligible in three categories: 205 GTI 1.9 'Challenge' specification, Group N 1.6 GTI and Group N 205 Rallye (1,300cc). The formula was altered with a mid-season split into a Masters category for the top five drivers and the Challenge for the remaining competitors. It was David Higgins, younger brother of the Manx rally driver Mark, who led the series at the halfway mark, supported by a team comprising most of the personnel behind Richard Burns'

Paul Frankland takes off at one of the many jumps on the Circuit of Ireland rally, in 1990, in his works Group A 205 GTI 1.9.

efforts two years previously. He also finished highest at the end of the season, but when a controversial technical infringement was found on his car, the Championship prize money and the works RAC drive were awarded to runner-up Mark Lawn. 1993 also saw the final outings for works-entered 205 GTIs on the RAC rally, the new 306 being used from the 1994 event onwards.

As this book is being written, the Peugeot Rally Club continues to provide the up-and-coming rally stars of the future with the best possible platform, the only change from the original concept in 1984 being the predominant use of the 106 Rallye and 306 S16 models.

On track

Despite the 205's obvious suitability for motorsport, and hence its mammoth success in the rallying world, the circuit racing potential of the car was almost overlooked. Although the 1,600cc GTI was competitive in its class, the 1.9 version was up against larger cars with 2 litres and 16 valves, such as the Vauxhall Astra and Volkswagen Golf 16v. Nevertheless, Peugeot retained an involvement in saloon car racing in 1987 with the support of four cars in the Monroe Shock Absorber Production Saloon Car Championship, one of whose drivers was the late Kieth Odor, who later would make his mark in both the British and German Touring Car Championships prior to his fatal accident in the latter. At the end of 1987, David Oates came third overall in Class C of the Monroe series with his Group N 205 GTI 1.9.

It was the advent of the larger 309 GTI and the introduction of the 160bhp 16-valve version of it that reduced the popularity of the 205 GTI for circuit racing. Subsequently, however, it has proved to be an ideal choice for the Slick 50 Road Saloon Car Championship, being both competitive in its class and cheap to prepare.

A 20-year-old Richard Burns pictured at the end of 1990 with his trophies and Peugeot's former Director of Motorsport, Des O'Dell.

A Peugeot GTI Rally Challenge competitor in the 1,600cc category on the Imber Stages rally, at Salisbury Plain in April 1990.

Richard Burns and co-driver Robert Reid on their way to a Challenge victory in the Ardennes rally in Belgium, in March 1991.

Not every Peugeot Rally Challenge competitor has all the luck, but with a full rollcage the driver and co-driver were unscathed after this nasty roll.

In France, the 205 Rallye, unsurprisingly, is a more popular car to use for rallying.

Although this rally car is a 1.9 GTI, the wheelarch trim is obviously from a 205 Rallye and the larger rear spoiler is from a kit.

Above: Being a mechanic on the Peugeot Rally Challenge is a labour of love, especially when repairing muddy cars in makeshift car parks in the middle of nowhere!

Top right: The 205 was not as popular on the track as in the forests, but it does make a good racing car for events like the Slick 50 Road Saloon Car Championship.

Right: One event of the 1992 Challenge calendar was not a rally, but a circuit race, which was held in pouring rain at Donington Park.

After the Group B rally cars had been banned at the end of 1986, they quickly reappeared in rallycross specification and the Brands Hatch and Lydden circuits in Kent were often the scene of a T16 in action, right through into the Nineties. Scandinavians Seppo Niittymaki and Terje Schie took several class victories with the T16 and T16 E2, while a 205 GTI in the hands of a young Johnny Milner had some success in its class. Rear-wheel drive makes a better rallycross car in the absence of four-wheel drive, and it has even been known to convert a 205 GTI to this drive layout with a rear-mounted Opel Manta 400 engine!

CHAPTER 9

Getting the best out of your 205

Ownership and modifications

What to buy?

The question 'What to buy?' is usually folllowed by 'What to spend?'. The sporting models ceased production at the end of 1993 and in early 1997 a secondhand GTI could range from less than £1,000 for a 1984 or 1985 1.6 model in poor condition to £10,000 for a '1 FM' limited-edition or a mint 1994 CTI. Unless you are either choosy or good at hunting, the T16 and Rallye derivatives are unlikely to be available on the UK secondhand market. In any case, with less than 30 T16s rumoured to remain in the world, their secondhand value is difficult to ascertain, but certainly it must be in excess of £30,000. The Rallye model, also made in left-hand-drive form only, was produced from 1985 to 1992, and it should be possible to import examples from less than £2,000 upwards.

The 1,360cc XS and GT models, also the D Turbo derivatives, are very attractive to the secondhand buyer and generally fetch the same price as, or perhaps even a little more than, a GTI in similar condition. The GTI therefore, is the most obvious choice for the performance enthusiast, and there are plenty to choose from. If insurance is a consideration, it is worth getting a quote to see if it is worth looking for a 1.6 GTI or maybe considering a XS, itself a very capable car and deceptively fast. The Peugeot Sport Club has an insurance scheme which will bring the possibility of GTI ownership (and its group 12 insurance rating) within reach of even 17-year-olds.

1.6 or 1.9?

This is the hardest choice, mainly because the 1.6 version is such a good car. Indeed, many drivers have rated the 1.6 a better driver's car, offering more fun in its handling and a more responsive engine. However, ownership of such a car is likely to make the heart yearn for the more powerful version. The 1.9, of course, will have larger and arguably more attractive wheels and half-leather upholstery, but these could be added to a 1.6 version without too much difficulty. The 1.9 has against it a higher insurance rating (group 14) and a slightly higher (about 5 per cent) purchase price, but other running costs, including fuel, will be surprisingly similar.

For both models, there will be a wide choice of cars at all price points. However, there will be good cars, owned by enthusiasts and having a full history, and there will be poor cars, that have been badly maintained and abused. Many will have had accident damage, too. It is therefore wise to buy a car of this kind primarily on condition and history rather than on its year of registration.

For less than £2,500, it should be possible to buy a nice post-1986 1.6 model with the 115bhp engine; similar money should purchase an early 1.9. If a 1.9 is your clear choice, it is worth looking for a post-1988 car, with the later design of dashboard, although this applies equally to the 1.6. The second major facelift hurdle came in September 1990, so a 1991 car, in either engine size, will represent the latest specification.

Additionally, the three most desirable colours were then available as an option: Sorrento Green, Miami Blue and Steel Grey. These match the character of the car without having the popularity of white and red. Additionally, the

The engine bay of a standard GTI 1.6. Not all are as well-maintained as this example, so look carefully for signs of neglect.

Mirrors on cars before 1987 were of this design rather than being more rectangular. A useful dating point.

Sorrento Green and Steel Grey models have a much more tasteful interior, with green and black seats as opposed to red and black, and dark green carpeting rather than red. Power steering and ABS were available as an option, and although rarely specified, they are worth looking around for as they greatly increase the pleasure and safety of the car. 1993 cars were only made in a 1.9 version with a standard catalyst, which performs only marginally better than a 1.6, but with worse fuel consumption. Therefore, a late 1992 car in the colours mentioned represents the pinnacle, with one exception. At the beginning of 1990, the 1,200 Limited Edition models were launched in Miami Blue and Sorrento Green, and with their superior specification, including full-leather upholstery and power-assisted steering, are the most sought-after, with a price premium of around £1,000 over equivalent standard models.

Convertible models are much rarer and are best bought towards the end of the winter, when they will be around 5 per cent cheaper. There is little point in spending more just to get the larger 1.9 engine as it produced less power than

the 1.6 version, but the standard electric hood fitted as standard from 1991 may prove beneficial. The rarity value of these cars inflates the price tremendously, and an average-condition 1987 car will fetch almost £3,000, with the last L-registration cars able to command almost three times that. At its peak, however, a new model was listed at just short of £15,000! The CJ model is particularly popular, and used prices can be higher than for the CTI. Despite its low power (1.4-litre engine) and basic (Junior) specification, used examples from 1989 can fetch nearly £4,000. A plus side of buying a convertible model is that they have often been kept as a second car, and consequently the average mileage tends to be lower, but on the other hand, due to the nature of convertible cars, it is more likely to have had several owners.

What to look for
As with any hot hatch, a used example is likely to have been driven hard and also may have sustained accident damage at some time in its life. If it has been repaired well, this will be

This shape of rear spoiler gave way to a new design in 1988. A pre-1988 car with a new-style spoiler is a clue to a car that has had a rear-end accident.

Fading bumpers and rusty driving lamps may seem unsightly, but they can always be replaced, and meanwhile they give a clue that this car is original and has had no accident repairs.

Wider-section 195/50 tyres and a Sebring performance exhaust transforms the rear appearance of a GTI. A small part of the rear valance has been trimmed away to accommodate the larger tailpipe.

difficult to spot, but it should not cause too much concern; it is the poorly repaired cars that should be avoided. Signs of frontal damage may be established by looking along the join where the front wing is bonded inside the bonnet opening. If opposite sides are different, or there is fresh bonding, there has been a new wing. Secondly, the shade of the plastic bumpers and trim went from grey to dark grey (almost black) in September 1990, and cars made before this, but repaired subsequently, will have darker bumpers. Tatty, faded plastic trim at least indicates an original car, despite the appearance. There are plenty of valet products, though, for bringing new life to old trim. At the back of the car, a pre-1988 model with the later straight tailgate spoiler will be a giveaway sign of a replacement part. Lifting the boot carpet may also show evidence of repair. The front spotlights will also be looking tired if they are more than five years old.

Rust is one thing that 205s are particularly good at avoiding; even a 10-year-old car can be totally free of rust. Areas to check are around all window edges, especially

There are many aftermarket parts available to improve the look of the 205, including this roof spoiler from Gutmann.

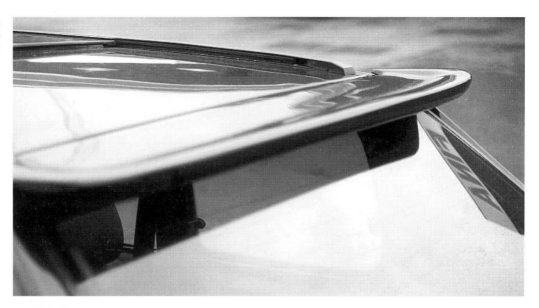

When the standard stereo system doesn't suffice, the boot is the obvious place to build a sound system, as in this Gutmann 205.

Rolling-road tuning is the best way to ensure that a car is producing the brake horsepower it was designed to deliver.

under the seals, and around the sill area. At the front of the car, the spoiler, grille and bumper are all plastic.

The chassis plate is clearly mounted in the engine bay – check this against the registration document, and have an 'HPI' check to be sure that the car is no longer part of a finance agreement, or has been written-off previously.

The remainder of the car's exterior is down to the eye, but internally, expect the side bolsters of the driver's seat to be worn down and pedal rubbers equally worn. The rest of the interior should be smart, but replacement items are easy to come by at secondhand parts dealers. Typically, a replacement driver's seat should cost around £50.

Parts for the GTI models are not too expensive and are readily available from Peugeot dealers. Also, a large supply of copy parts should be available at many outlets. Prices of parts are reasonable, with an alloy wheel costing around £100 in 1997, an exhaust £180, an exchange starter motor £90, a clutch £90 and a windscreen £110, right down to an oil filter at £7. Peugeot have around 400 dealer franchises in the UK, and many more throughout Europe.

Turning to mechanical condition, an engine should always start first time, but don't expect the tickover to be perfect; this was an inherent fault on the cars, and poor tickover and stalling can occur for a number of reasons. There are also many old wives' tales as to the best solution, but a visit to a Bosch dealer (makers of the car's fuel injection system) with

their specialist diagnostic equipment can usually identify and sort the problem.

The most important part of any service history is evidence of a cam belt change. A fully stamped service booklet is insufficient proof; it is important to see evidence of a receipted invoice. The reason for this is that Peugeot do not stipulate its change in the service requirements, but nevertheless it should be done every 48,000 miles. The part costs around £10, and the work takes just over two hours to complete. Remember that a broken cam belt can do hundreds of pounds' worth of damage to the engine.

Join the Club

Surely the ownership of any car cannot be complete for the true enthusiast without membership of the corresponding owners' club. In the UK, there is a choice of two clubs, one of which is aimed fairly and squarely at the sporting Peugeot owner.

The Peugeot Sport Club started life in 1985 as the Peugeot 205 GTI Club. It was conceived by Peugeot's own

Des O'Dell, the retired Director of Motorsport for Peugeot, is the Peugeot Sport Club's President. He had much influence on the Turbo 16 project and on the similarity of the GTI styling to that of the Turbo 16.

At the Peugeot Sport Club's annual National Convention there is the opportunity to take a 205 (or any other sporting Peugeot) around a racing circuit.

sales and marketing department when just the 205 GTI 1.6 was on sale, but soon there were around 1,500 members. Not since the Sixties had there been so many tales of drivers acknowledging each other by a flash of the headlights, such was this recognition of camaraderie. It was an ideal scenario for an owners' club, and a thriving one at that. In 1987 the club was renamed the Peugeot GTI Club, to reflect the introduction of the 309 GTI, and now it welcomes owners of all sporting Peugeots.

For a modest subscription currently of £15 and a once-only joining fee of £5, members receive a quarterly magazine, *Torque*, and their membership card entitles the holder to a 10 per cent discount on parts and labour at approximately half of the Peugeot dealerships in the UK, as well as some parts and tuning outlets. Additionally, the Club's insurance scheme is highly competitive as enthusiastic car-owning club members historically are a better risk than the average policy-holder, and therefore premiums can be cheaper. Details of discounts are published regularly in the magazine, which also has information on new Peugeot models, Peugeot motorsport activities and a lively letters page.

A major focus for members is the National Convention, held annually at various prestigious venues, including the Silverstone circuit in Northamptonshire. The place comes alive as members drive their own car around the track,

The car park at the Peugeot Sport Club National Convention is packed full with over 300 sporting Peugeots, predominantly the 205 GTI.

The track sessions at the National Convention are a wonderful sight, with many 205s being driven with great enthusiasm and enjoyment.

polish them for the *Concours d'Elegance* and take part in a whole host of other activities. In addition, local groups meet throughout the year and offer the chance to exchange views with other members. It is certainly not a club for the 'anorak brigade', and it offers sporting Peugeot drivers the chance to make real savings and gain the most enjoyment from their car.

The other club for Peugeot owners is Club Peugeot UK, which has been established for many years and caters for owners of all models including some dating back to prewar. There is a good balance between old and new, and this club has a relaxed and friendly atmosphere, with a particularly strong social aspect. Around the world, there is a strong

following of the marque as a whole, witness the Peugeot Sport Club in Holland, Club Peugeot GTI in France and an active local club, the Cabourg 205 GTI Club, in northern France. If you have difficulty in contacting one of the British clubs, an up-to-date contact address is available by telephoning the Customer Relations department at Peugeot's UK Head Office.

Mechanical modifications

Many owners seem to believe that in order to increase the enjoyment of their car, it is essential that they fit it with a 16-valve 405 Mi16 engine. Desirable, perhaps, but certainly not essential, which is just as well for anyone on a tight

If 160bhp is still not enough, the addition of Weber Twin 45 carburettors, as fitted to this car, takes the power output to over 200bhp.

budget. In any case, an engine transplant alone is insufficient – and potentially dangerous – because any performance enhancements from the engine must be matched by appropriate improvements in the car's braking and handling performance.

The first step in tuning a 205 GTI must be to ensure that the car is producing the brake horsepower that it was designed to, namely a true 104 or 114bhp for a 1.6, and 128bhp for a 1.9. By taking the car to a rolling road, where a tuning session should cost around £60, it should be possible to get quite close to the correct output figure. About 125bhp from a 1.9 is quite respectable and is equivalent to around 99bhp at the wheels.

New spark plugs (note that the three engines mentioned in the previous paragraph all take different plugs) will do no harm (at around £7 for a set of four) and a change to fully synthetic oil in both engine and gearbox, though it will not alter the total bhp output from the engine, will increase the power available at the wheels by a few bhp as rolling resistance is reduced. However, fully synthetic oil must not be confused with synthetic-based or semi-synthetic oils, which are not the same. Most motor accessory shops now sell this oil, and a 5-litre can, costing around £20, should be just enough. Fully synthetic gearbox oil is harder to find, but many prestige manufacturers use this as standard and hence their dealerships will be stockists.

When considering an engine conversion or modification, remember that drivability is more important than maximum brake horsepower figures, also be wary of any claimed figures. Some manufacturers tend to be very optimistic, whereas some others have been known to offer a money-back guarantee if the customer is not satisfied with the conversion. Some of the modifications listed below will offer an improvement of perhaps only 1-2bhp, and when combined with another modification, for example a performance air filter along with a fuel pressure regulator, may not result in a power increase equal to the sum of those available from the individual parts. Purists may also like to know that blueprinting the XU engine makes only a small difference as the tolerances in the design and manufacture of the engine are already very fine.

Air filter modifications are available from K&N, and Piper and JR Filters make replacement elements. The 57i filter kit from K&N provides a more direct route for the induction, removing the need for much of the hosing under the bonnet. The cone filter sits behind the left headlight and the kit is very easy to fit, and competitively priced. It should be noted that this corner of the engine bay may already have been used for a retro-fit alarm or power-steering reservoir if PAS was fitted as an option.

A replacement exhaust will be necessary on most 205s after around 70,000 miles and a performance aftermarket

Team Hartwell can fit a very neatly installed Mi16 engine under the bonnet of a 205.

system should cost only a fraction more than a standard part from either a Peugeot dealer or a while-you-wait exhaust centre. These exhausts may be a little louder, but they do tend to produce a nice sound. Sebring, Remus, Ansa and Jetex all produce a range of exhausts that vary in noise level – the choice is very much a subjective matter, but my personal favourite happens to be the Sebring model with an oval chromed tailpipe. If you are looking for lifetime performance, Magnex, whose exhausts have been fitted to Peugeots competing in the British Touring Car Championship, also make models for the 205.

Modifications have an element of fashion, and the influence of motor racing, in particular the German Touring Car Championship (DTM) has spawned an array of DTM-style exhausts, with twin tailpipes upswept for the last 2 inches. Many exhausts will require a minor modification to the rear valance to stop the tailpipe rubbing; this may be achieved with a sharp knife or junior hacksaw. Incidentally, the exhaust manifold that Peugeot fitted as standard is so good that replacement is not necessary at this stage.

Reprogramming of the engine control unit (ECU), otherwise known as 'chipping', is highly effective on turbocharged cars, but has a different purpose on a 205. Whilst a reprogrammed chip will produce an additional 2-3bhp right across the middle and upper rev-ranges, it is the biggest cure for the driveline shunt and 'kangarooing' that affects the GTI models. Companies such as Superchips and BBR (Starchip) were quoting less than £200 in 1997 to exchange an ECU, but there will also be a small, but worthwhile, price to pay at the petrol pumps. Another method of sending differing amounts of fuel to the engine is via a fuel pressure regulator, but again this will have an effect on fuel consumption when delivering increased performance.

Tyres and wheels can make a huge difference to the 205, as exemplary handling is there to be taken. Owners of the 1.6 GTI model can benefit from fitting the larger 15in rims from the 1.9. Incidentally, both designs of GTI alloy wheel will fit on lesser three-door models, even though the rear wheelarch design is different on the GTI. The first step for the 1.9 owner is to replace the 185/55VR-15 rubber with 195/50VR-15 all round. Being a more common size, these tyres are usually cheaper, have an almost identical rolling circumference, and transform the handling. It is worth checking, though, that satisfactory clearance is maintained in the rear wheelarches, especially when the car is heavily laden.

For a more personal look, or the desire to use even larger wheels, there are a choice of styles of up to 17in diameter which will fit inside the standard arches, although the grey plastic wheelarch trims may need to be trimmed within the arches to avoid clearance problems.

If you are preparing for a serious power increase, the car's braking capabilities must be similarly uprated. Having already fitted at least 195/50-section tyres, the next step should be a set of performance brake pads, such as Mintex M171s. Remember, though, that there may be a slight trade-off in 'cold' performance against their anti-fade superiority over standard pads when warmed-up. For a further improvement in braking performance upgraded front discs are the answer, either the drilled type as made by Brembo, or grooved discs, which Tarox offer with a choice of either 12 or 40 grooves. There is little need to change the discs at the back, but braided hoses and dot-5 racing fluid are further steps towards improved braking worth considering.

Peugeot designed the suspension of the GTI to be uprated and lowered, but there is ample scope for lowering the car further, either because of the desire to improve handling at the expense of ride quality, or for aesthetic reasons, or even both! Springs may be shortened and torsion bars may be adjusted to provide lower ride heights, but kits are available which offer adjustable settings. Suppliers who make performance springs and shock absorbers for the 205 include Jamex, Spax, Pi and de Carbon.

Uprated power

For those with a 1.6-litre GTI, or even a lesser model, the obvious route to 130bhp is to fit a 1.9-litre GTI engine. Because of the lower gearing of the 1.6, a car modified in this way will accelerate even quicker than a standard 1.9. There is an ample supply of these engines from cars that have been either written-off or given an engine transplant themselves. It should be possible to complete a 1.9 conversion from around £700, but this does not include the cost of the braking and suspension modifications to complement the extra power.

There are several ways of increasing power beyond the 130bhp starting point, so it is best to take advice from the various tuning companies as to what can be achieved within a specified budget, remembering again that some of the money should be reserved for other parts of the car. Different cams, modified cylinder heads and twin carburettors can all be used to bring useful power gains to the eight-valve engines, but only if the various modifications chosen complement each other satisfactorily to give a balanced result.

Serious power
Rather than modify the existing engine to increase the power output it may be easier to fit a more powerful engine. The 160bhp 1,905cc 16-valve engine from the Peugeot 405 Mi16 (also found in the Citroen BX GTi 16-valve) is ideal for a transplant, and secondhand engines can be fitted from around £1,000. The tuning can then start on this engine, with reprogrammed ECUs, wilder cams and even twin carburettors making 200bhp a possibility without compromising drivability. The newer 2-litre 16-valve engine from the Peugeot 306 S16 (and the Citroen ZX 16-valve) is

The Gutmann Turbo 8S engine was a very expensive but magical way to increase performance; coupled to higher gearing, this car is capable of over 145mph.

similar, and its power output of 155bhp can immediately be raised with the removal of the catalytic converter and the fitment of a performance exhaust, making 170bhp an easy target. The engine in the newest 306, the GTI-6, produces 167bhp in standard form, so there is even more to play with!

The Turbo Technics conversion mentioned in Chapter 5 offered 175bhp and some early 205s were fitted with superchargers, but their reliability was suspect and both of these routes required a very low-mileage engine as a base, something which is now difficult to find. Perhaps the most effective way to achieve serious power is by using one of Peugeot's own turbocharged engines. The 'mild' turbo, producing 150bhp, can be found in the 406, 605 and 806 (though not in the last case in the UK) and the ECU can be reprogrammed to produce anything up to

Twin headlamps come in two varieties – this version having relocated indicators to allow for larger headlights.

In addition to the many aftermarket body kits, it is possible to modify the bumper and spoiler from a 309 GTI to fit the 205 and have driving lamps and foglamps.

Several different styles of front grille are available from tuning companies.

Among other modifications, this 205 has a front splitter assembly adapted from a Renault Laguna. Parts from a Vauxhall Calibra are also suitable.

This car is fitted with a body kit from Fibresports – providing an attractive appearance for the budget-conscious.

200bhp without a problem. The very rare 220bhp 16-valve turbocharged engine from the 405 Turbo 16 will also fit, and an example has been made producing a comfortable 240bhp. One of the range of engine conversions available from Gutmann in the early Nineties was the Turbo 8S, producing over 170bhp, but with the turbocharger coming on boost from as little as 1,900rpm. This enabled the car's gearing to be raised, and a top speed of over 145mph was possible. However, this was not a cheap option.

When considering a major boost in power, traction will always be an issue, but this can be addressed by conversion to four-wheel drive. This may not seem possible in a car like the 205, but with a little time, and several of the parts from a four-wheel-drive 405 Mi16x4, it can be achieved. This then begs the question of what to put under the bonnet, and surprisingly the answer could be a Ford engine, not one from Peugeot. The 2-litre Ford Cosworth YB engine will fit

This 205 GTI has a Gutmann grille and front spoiler, in addition to a turbocharged engine producing over 180bhp.

A Gutmann 'Turbo Look ' kit with twin headlamps and colour-coded door mirrors.

Another Gutmann body kit with twin lamps and colour-coded bumpers with black inserts.

(longitudinally for four-wheel drive) and it can be tuned to in excess of 400bhp. If that's not enough ...

Optical tuning

A more insurance-friendly way of giving a 205 individuality is to change its appearance. One of the easiest ways to freshen-up an old GTI (or any other model) is to fit the clear front indicator lenses (less than £20 a pair at the time of writing) and perhaps change the colour of the bumper and trim inserts. Twin round headlights (available in two designs – one with indicators in the front bumper) or headlamp 'lightbrows' can also alter the look of the front of a 205. Many owners have replaced the rather ugly square side repeater indicators with oval ones (available at all good

The Gutmann 'Turbo Look' kit does away with all the plastic bumper and door trim (and even one of the plastic rear-quarter badges) to create a smoother look to the body.

The Peugeot body kit complements the car well and is quite durable. This car has one of the most sought-after registration marks for a Peugeot.

The Gutmann 'Race Look 2' kits were very popular at the beginning of the Nineties, and this *Concours d'Elegance* entrant has also specified matching Gutmann wheels. The car at the rear of the picture has alloy wheels originally found on Peugeot's 405 Mi16.

Body kits can be mixed. Here, the Peugeot front spoiler matches the Zender side skirts, with 16-inch Dimma three-piece split-rim alloy wheels filling the arches nicely.

Ford dealers!) and at the back, light lenses can be tinted black to good effect. Headlamp protective covers help to maintain the look of a 205 and are available as a dealer accessory.

One of the most popular accessories when the 205 was new was a reflective rear tailgate panel in place of the grey slats. This gave the car a nice look, but fashions change, and it is more popular now to either colour-code the panel or possibly remove it altogether and have the tailgate completely body-coloured. Dimma offer an authentic racing fuel cap trim inexpensively to brighten up the rear quarter-panel. Lastly, graphics can also personalize the look of a car, with well-chosen locations on the body for the 205 and lion symbols, while for white cars in particular, Peugeot Talbot Sport stripes give the car a 'rally' appearance.

For a total transformation, a wide bodykit might be the answer. Many of those produced replicated the shape of the Turbo 16, but only the genuine Dimma kit has stood the test of time. The word Dimma has become synonymous with wide-arched Peugeots. The original package was not cheap at around £5,000, but it included the full kit, fitted and painted, along with 16in split rims, which were remarkably similar in styling to those on the standard 1.9. The choice of colours was astounding and the paint finish was of an extremely high standard. A kit was also available for the 205 Convertible.

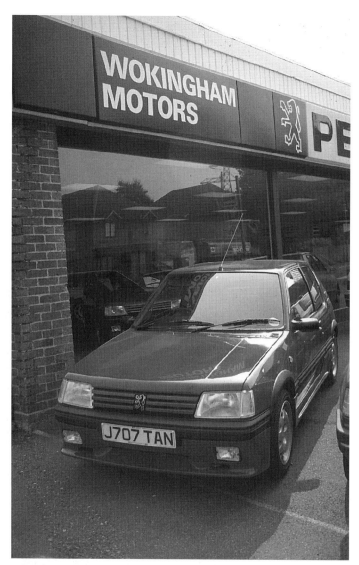

Dealers can easily fit a Peugeot body kit from their accessory catalogue.

Wheels are a personal choice for a 205 owner. The car in the foreground has a set of understated Speedline 7x15 alloys from the Peugeot Talbot Sport Special Tuning department; the car on the right has five-spoke 7x15 Gutmann alloys.

Colour-coding is a popular way of making a 205 look different. This owner has extended the theme to the wheels and completed the look with GTI mudflaps.

For anyone seeking something a little milder, the choice is astronomical, and a £500 budget should give an owner a wide choice. Peugeot produced a kit themselves, comprising a front spoiler, side skirts, a rear valance and an optional boot spoiler. Other good-value kits include those made by KAT, RGM, Zender (as on the front cover) and Fibresports.

A more recent trend to achieve individuality has been to obtain a kit from Europe, which is therefore rarer in the UK. From France, stunning kits are available from P A Tuning and Esquiss Autos, while Germany produce kits coutesy of Musketier and Postert. Many of these are now imported professionally into the UK. For high quality, but at a more expensive price, Gutmann make a choice of body kits and accessories for all Peugeot models. Their products are very solid and complement the car very well, their 'Race Look 2' kit being particularly popular.

Trends do come and go with body styling, and some of the styling cues from racing cars often find their way onto the tuning scene. One such example is the front splitter,

Despite the lowered suspension of this Gutmann model, there is room under the wheelarches for 17-inch Minilite alloys, painted in this instance in a bottle green colour to match the bumpers and trim.

Cleaning the alloy wheels is part of 205 ownership. If the wheels are kept free of brake dust and cleaned regularly they set off the appearance of the whole car.

originally seen in the German Touring Car race series, and now available from companies like DTM Technic for certain Peugeot models, including the 205.

Whether you are looking for just a different style of front grille, or perhaps a larger T16-style rear spoiler, a vast choice is still available for the 205, even though the car has ceased production.

Interior improvements

With so much scope for modifications to the exterior and in the engine bay, it is important that the interior of any modified car should not be overlooked. The seats of a 1.6 GTI or an XS or GT model can quite easily be replaced by the half-leather trimmed 1.9 GTI seats; keep looking around for cars that are being dismantled, but do not expect to find a bargain. The full-leather seats from the 1990 Limited Edition are even more sought after. The sports seats from a Peugeot 306 also fit, as do certain seats made by companies like Recaro.

Owners may like to add a sunroof, central locking or electric windows, if not already fitted, and of course many will wish to upgrade the In Car Entertainment (ICE) equipment, but that is a subject dominated by personal taste. Lastly, the personal touch can continue to be added inside with white or coloured dashboard graphics, alloy pedals, different gear-knobs and steering wheels, all items

A spare wheel lock, available as a Peugeot dealer accessory, is essential to stop the risk of theft with alloy wheels. For the same reason, locking nuts for the road wheels are highly recommended. A number of different systems are on the market.

If you don't care for Peugeot's standard seating it is possible to fit a pair of Recaros like these, which are electrically adjustable and have a memory setting.

which are well publicized for the 205 in tuning magazines not only in the UK, but throughout much of Europe, where there is even more choice.

Security

To protect a high-performance car like a sporting 205, alarms and immobilizers must be considered. Many insurance companies insist on GTI models being retro-fitted with an immobilizer, often to Thatcham Category 1 standard, and of course an alarm is the best way to deter a potential break-in. A tracking device is also a sensible option if the vehicle is particularly special or has a high sentimental value as 98 per cent of vehicles fitted with such a device are claimed to be recovered. A set of locking wheel nuts is also essential, not forgetting the vulnerable spare wheel, which should either have a lock fitted (available for around £45 from Peugeot dealers) or be kept in the boot.

A list of useful addresses for Peugeot enthusiasts and owners seeking to maintain and/or improve their sporting 205 will be found in a following Appendix.

A huge array of 205 models is available to the collector.

Tailpiece: the Peugeot 205 GTI, with its stylish looks, sharp handling and exhilarating performance, has brought delight to many owners and a rejuvenated image to its manufacturer.

APPENDIX A

Technical specifications

205 GTI 1.6

Engine: Four-cylinder, in-line, aluminium block with replaceable liners, aluminium alloy cylinder head. Five main bearings. Single overhead camshaft driven by toothed belt. Bosch L-Jetronic fuel injection.
- 1984-1986 (Type XU5J 180A)
1,580cc, bore 83mm, stroke 73mm, compression ratio 10.2:1. 105bhp (DIN) at 6,250rpm, 99lb.ft at 4,000rpm.
- 1986-1992 (Type XU5JA B6D)
1,580cc, bore 83mm, stroke 73mm, compression ratio 9.8:1. 115bhp (DIN) at 6,250rpm, 98lb.ft at 4,000rpm.
Transmission: Five-speed, all indirect, with synchromesh.
Ratios (mph per 1,000rpm): 1st 3.31 (4.9); 2nd 1.88 (8.6); 3rd 1.36 (11.9); 4th 1.07 (15.2); 5th 0.87 (18.7). Final-drive ratio 4.06:1.
Suspension: Front: Independent with MacPherson struts, coil springs, lower wishbones and anti-roll bar. Rear: Independent with trailing arms, transverse torsion bars, telescopic shock absorbers and anti-roll bar.
Steering: Rack and pinion, 3.2 turns from lock to lock.
Brakes: Front: 9.7in diameter ventilated discs. Rear: 7.1in diameter drums. Vacuum servo.
Wheels: 5.5J-14in diameter cast-alloy, with 185/60HR-14 radial-ply tyres. Tyre pressures 29psi front and rear.
Capacities: Fuel tank: 11.0 gallons (50 litres). Cooling system: 11.5 pints (6.5 litres). Engine sump: 5 pints (2.85 litres).
Dimensions: Overall length: 145.9in. Overall width: 61.9in. Overall height: 53.3in. Wheelbase: 95.3in. Front track: 54.8in. Rear track: 52.3in. Maximum payload: 937lb. Kerb weight: 1,874lb.

205 CTI

Engine: Four-cylinder, in-line, aluminium block with replaceable liners, aluminium alloy cylinder head. Five main bearings. Single overhead camshaft driven by toothed belt. Bosch L-Jetronic fuel injection.
- 1986-1991 (Type XU5JA B6D)

1,580cc, bore 83mm, stroke 73mm, compression ratio 9.8:1. 115bhp (DIN) at 6,250rpm, 98lb.ft at 4,000rpm.
- 1991-1994 (Type XU9JI/Z)
1,905cc, bore 83mm, stroke 88mm, compression ratio 8.4:1. 105bhp (DIN) at 6,000rpm, 101lb.ft at 4,000rpm.
Transmission: Five-speed, all indirect, with synchromesh.
Ratios (mph per 1,000rpm): 1st 3.31 (4.9); 2nd 1.88 (8.6); 3rd 1.36 (11.9); 4th 1.07 (15.2); 5th 0.87 (18.7). Final-drive ratio 4.06:1.
Suspension: Front: Independent with MacPherson struts, coil springs and anti-roll bar. Rear: Independent with trailing arms, transverse torsion bars, telescopic shock absorbers and anti-roll bar.
Steering: Rack and pinion, 3.2 turns from lock to lock.
Brakes: Front: 9.7in diameter ventilated discs. Rear: 7.1in diameter drums. Vacuum servo.
Wheels: 5.5J-14in diameter cast-alloy, with 185/60HR-14 radial-ply tyres. Tyre pressures 29psi front and rear.
Capacities: Fuel tank: 11.0 gallons (50 litres). Cooling system: 11.5 pints (6.5 litres). Engine sump: 8.8 pints (5.0 litres).
Dimensions: Overall length: 145.9in. Overall width: 62.6in. Overall height: 54.4in. Wheelbase: 95.3in. Front track: 54.8in. Rear track: 52.3in. Maximum payload: 1,030lb. Kerb weight: 2,062lb.

205 GTI 1.9

Engine: Four-cylinder, in-line, aluminium block with replaceable liners, aluminium alloy cylinder head. Five main bearings. Single overhead camshaft driven by toothed belt. Bosch L-Jetronic fuel injection.
- 1986-1993 (Type XU9JA)
1,905cc, bore 83mm, stroke 88mm, compression ratio 9.6:1. 130bhp (DIN) at 6,000rpm, 119lb.ft at 4,750rpm.
- 1990-1994 (Type XU9JAZ) (catalyst-equipped)
1,905cc, bore 83mm, stroke 88mm, compression ratio 9.2:1. 122bhp (DIN) at 6,000rpm, 111lb.ft at 4,000rpm.
Transmission: Five-speed, all indirect, with synchromesh.

Ratios (mph per 1,000rpm): 1st 2.92 (6.2); 2nd 1.85 (9.8); 3rd 1.36 (13.3); 4th 1.07 (16.9); 5th 0.86 (20.9). Final-drive ratio 3.69:1.
Suspension: Front: Independent with MacPherson struts, coil springs, lower wishbones and anti-roll bar. Rear: Independent with trailing arms, transverse torsion bars, telescopic shock absorbers and anti-roll bar.
Steering: Rack and pinion, 3.2 turns from lock to lock.
Brakes: Front: 9.7in diameter ventilated discs. Rear: 7.1in diameter solid discs. Vacuum servo.
Wheels: 5.5J-14in diameter cast-alloy, with 185/60HR-14 radial-ply tyres. Tyre pressures 29psi front and rear.
Capacities: Fuel tank: 11.0 gallons (50 litres). Cooling system: 11.6 pints (6.6 litres). Engine sump: 8.8 pints (5.0 litres).
Dimensions: Overall length: 145.9in. Overall width: 61.9in. Overall height: 53.3in. Wheelbase: 95.3in. Front track: 54.4in. Rear track: 52.7in. Maximum payload: 960lb. Kerb weight: 1,929lb.

205 Rallye

Engine: Four-cylinder, in-line, aluminium block with replaceable liners, aluminium alloy cylinder head. Five main bearings. Single overhead camshaft driven by toothed belt. Two twin-choke Weber 40 DCOM 10 carburettors.
Type TU24 – 1,294cc, bore 75mm, stroke 73.2mm, compression ratio 9.6:1. 103bhp (DIN) at 6,800rpm, 88lb.ft at 5,000rpm.
Transmission: Five-speed, all indirect, with synchromesh.
Mph per 1,000rpm: 1st (4.4); 2nd (7.7); 3rd (11.2); 4th (14.3); 5th (17.7).
Suspension: Front: Independent with MacPherson struts, coil springs, lower wishbones and anti-roll bar. Rear: Independent with trailing arms, transverse torsion bars, telescopic shock absorbers and anti-roll bar.
Steering: Rack and pinion, 3.8 turns from lock to lock.
Brakes: Front: 9.7in diameter ventilated discs. Rear: 7.1in diameter drums. Vacuum servo.
Wheels: 5.5B-13in diameter steel, with 165/70HR-13 radial-ply tyres. Tyre pressures 33psi front and rear.
Capacities: Fuel tank: 11.0 gallons (50 litres). Cooling system: 9.7 pints (5.5 litres). Engine sump: 3.5 pints (1.99 litres).
Dimensions: Overall length: 145.9in. Overall width: 61.9in. Overall height: 54.1in. Wheelbase: 95.3in. Front track: 55.1in. Rear track: 52.6in. Maximum payload: 946lb. Kerb weight: 1,738lb.

205 XS and GT (1984-1992)

Engine: Four-cylinder, in-line, aluminium block with replaceable liners, aluminium alloy cylinder head. Five main bearings. Single overhead camshaft driven by toothed belt.
Type TU3 – 1,360cc, bore 75mm, stroke 77mm, compression ratio 9.3:1. 85bhp (DIN) at 6,400rpm, 85.4lb.ft at 4,000rpm.
Transmission: Five-speed, all indirect, with synchromesh.
Suspension: Front: Independent with MacPherson struts, coil springs, lower wishbones and anti-roll bar. Rear: Independent with trailing arms, transverse torsion bars, telescopic shock absorbers and anti-roll bar.
Steering: Rack and pinion, 3.8 turns from lock to lock.
Brakes: Front: 9.7in diameter solid discs. Rear: 7.1in diameter drums. Vacuum servo.
Wheels: 5.5B-13in diameter steel, with 165/70SR-13 radial-ply tyres. Tyre pressures 29psi front and rear. Optional alloy wheels of same size.
Capacities: Fuel tank: 11.0 gallons (50 litres). Cooling system: 10.2 pints (5.8 litres). Engine sump: 4 pints (2.27 litres).
Dimensions: Overall length: 145.9in. Overall width: 61.9in. Overall height: 54.3in. Wheelbase: 95.3in. Front track: 55.1in. Rear track: 52.6in. Maximum payload: 935lb. Kerb weight: 1,804lb.

205 CJ (1988-1993)

Engine: Four-cylinder, in-line, aluminium block with replaceable liners, aluminium alloy cylinder head. Five main bearings. Single overhead camshaft driven by toothed belt. Two twin-choke Weber 40 DCOM 10 carburettors.
Type TU3A – 1,360cc, bore 75mm, stroke 73.2mm, compression ratio 9.3:1. 70bhp (DIN) at 5,600rpm, 81lb.ft at 3,400rpm.
Transmission: Five-speed, all indirect, with synchromesh.
Mph per 1,000rpm: 1st (5.0); 2nd (9.5); 3rd (13.5); 4th (17.6); 5th (22.4).
Suspension: Front: Independent with MacPherson struts, coil springs, lower wishbones and anti-roll bar. Rear: Independent with trailing arms, transverse torsion bars, telescopic shock absorbers and anti-roll bar.
Steering: Rack and pinion, 3.8 turns from lock to lock.
Brakes: Front: 9.7in diameter solid discs. Rear: 7.1in diameter drums. Vacuum servo.
Wheels: 5B-13in diameter steel, with 165/70R-13 radial-ply tyres. Tyre pressures 29psi front and rear.
Capacities: Fuel tank: 11.0 gallons (50 litres). Cooling system: 10.2 pints (5.8 litres). Engine sump: 4 pints (2.85 litres).
Dimensions: Overall length: 145.9in. Overall width: 61.9in. Overall height: 54.1in. Wheelbase: 95.3in. Front track: 55.1in. Rear track: 52.6in. Maximum payload: 946lb. Kerb weight: 1,738lb.

APPENDIX B

Production milestones

November 1982 – Production commences at Mulhouse, France.
February 1983 – 205 range launched in France, simultaneously with rally version, the 205 Turbo 16.
September 1983 – 205 range launched in UK.
April 1984 – 205 GTI 1.6 goes on sale in UK with price of £6,245.
December 1985 – Millionth 205 produced. Turbo 16 wins World Rally Championship.
June 1986 – 205 GTI 1.6 gains more powerful 115bhp engine and minor specification changes. Launch of 205 CTI in UK with price of £10,680.
December 1986 – More powerful 1.9 GTI goes on sale with 130bhp engine, higher level of specification and price of £8,445. Turbo 16 again wins World Rally Championship.
January 1987 – 205 Turbo 16 Grand Raid wins Paris-Dakar rally.
September 1987 – Two millionth 205 produced.
January 1988 – Major revision to entire 205 range including uprated 1,360cc engine, new dashboard and trim. Turbo 16 Grand Raid again wins Paris-Dakar rally.
March 1988 – 205 Rallye launched in Europe with 103bhp 1,294cc engine.
June 1988 – Launch of Cabriolet Junior (CJ) with 70bhp 1,360cc engine and price of £8,835.
May 1989 – Limited edition Roland Garros hatchback and Cabriolet launched.
June 1989 – Three millionth 205 produced.
August 1989 – Introduction of BE-3 gearbox and minor trim changes.
October 1989 – Limited edition of 1,200 Miami Blue and Sorrento Green models unveiled. Catalytic converter now an option on 1.9 GTI. Power-assisted steering optional on all GTI and CTI models.
December 1989 – Peugeot 205 named 'Car of the Decade' by *Car* magazine.
September 1990 – Revisions to plastic and trim colours and new front and rear light lenses. Electric hood standard on CTI. Anti-lock braking available as option on GTI models.

October 1990 – Limited edition GTI Griffe shown at Paris motor show.
December 1990 – 205 is Britain's 10th best-selling car in 1990, taking 2.5 per cent of UK market.
February 1991 – 1.8 D Turbo five-door launched with 78bhp 1,769cc turbodiesel engine and price of £10,703.
March 1991 – 205 Gentry revealed at Geneva motor show – 43rd official variant.
July 1991 – Four millionth 205 is produced. Over 300,000 models were GTIs and over 45,000 Cabriolets.
October 1991 – Catalyst engines fitted as standard to CJ (1,360cc producing 75bhp) and CTI (1,905cc producing 105bhp). Air conditioning now an option on GTI and CTI models. GTI models now have remote control central locking.
March 1992 – Limited edition 205 Gentry launched with automatic transmission, power-assisted steering and catalyst-equipped 105bhp 1,905cc engine at price of £12,836.
June 1992 – Limited edition UK-specification 205 Rallye, based on 1.1 Style, launched with 1,360cc 75bhp catalyst engine at cost of £7,995.
September 1992 – 205 GTI 1.6 ceases production with final UK price of £11,375.
October 1992 – Limited edition of just 25 205 GTI '1 FM' models launched to celebrate 25 years of Radio 1 with price of over £17,000, including £5,000 donation to charity.
October 1992 – GTI 1.9 now has 122bhp catalyst-equipped engine as standard and grey carpets.
October 1993 – Turbodiesel-powered STDT launched with GTI-style bodywork and alloy wheels with price of £9,860.
April 1994 – 205 GTI 1.9 and CTI cease production coinciding with the launch of sporting versions of 306 range. Final prices were £12,265 and £14,195, respectively.
February 1995 – Five millionth 205 produced.
1997 – 205 still being produced in a few variants.

APPENDIX C

Sales figures in the UK

	GTI models	Cabriolets	All models
1983	0	0	2,883
1984	1,874	0	19,670
1985	4,971	0	30,842
1986	7,378	427	39,188
1987	9,477	582	49,127
1988	10,933	1,020	54,147
1989	10,240	1,070	52,740
1990	8,324	1,274	50,205
1991	5,429	866	46,615
1992	2,498	549	34,045
1993	521	434	23,065
1994	8	11	10,694
1995	0	0	9,032
1996	0	0	3,046
Total	61,653	6,233	425,299

Peak year for GTI derivatives was 1988, taking over 20% of 205 UK sales. During 1991 the 205 range accounted for 3.08% of all UK registrations.

Included in the above totals are the following limited editions:
1990 – 600 Miami Blue 'Limited Edition' (300 1.6; 300 1.9)
1990 – 600 Sorrento Green 'Limited Edition' (300 1.6; 300 1.9)
1992/3 – 408 '205 Gentry' models
1992/3 – 25 'Radio 1FM' models

Global statistics:
Total GTI production:	332,942
Total Cabriolet production:	72,125
Total T16 production:	241
Total 205 production to end of 1996:	5,153,369

APPENDIX D

Useful addresses

Peugeot Motor Company, Aldermoor House, Aldermoor Lane, Coventry, West Midlands, CV3 1LT. Tel (01203) 884000.

Peugeot Sport Club, PO Box 405, Doncaster, South Yorkshire, DN4 8RS.

Club Peugeot UK, c/o Keith Herbert, 2 Sunnyside, Priors Hill, Timsbury, Bath, BA3 1HE. Tel (01761) 470246.

Musee Peugeot, Carrefour de l'Europe, 25600 Sochaux. Tel (00 33) 81 94 48 21.

Museum of British Road Transport, St Agnes Lane, Hales Street, Coventry, West Midlands, CV1 1PM. Tel (01203) 832425.

Chris Knott Insurance Consultants, Grove Mills, Cranbrook Road, Hawkhurst, Cranbrook, Kent, TN18 4AS. Tel (01580) 752961.

Privilege Insurance, 42 The Headrow, Leeds, LS1 8HZ. Tel (0113) 292 5555.

Peugeot Sport Special Tuning, PO Box 25, Humber Road, Coventry, CV3 1BD. Tel (01203) 884677. (*Competition and uprated road parts*)

ABP Motorsport, 416 Newcastle Road, Shavington, Crewe, Cheshire, CW2 5EB. Tel (01270) 67177. (*Performance parts*)

Andyspares Ltd, 13 Tessa Road, Reading, Berks, RG1 8HH. Tel (0118) 951 2828. (*Spare parts*)

Autocare, Prospect Mews, Prospect Street, Reading, Berks. Tel (0118) 958 9234. (*Servicing*)

Autofive, 5 Leftwich Warehouses, Queen Street, Northwich, Cheshire, CW9 5JN. Tel 07000 205484/Fax (01606) 42505. (*Replacement parts*)

BBR, Unit 1, Oxford Road, Brackley, Northants, NN13 7DY. Tel (01280) 702389. (*Modified ECUs*)

Carnoisseur, Brittany Court, High Street South, Dunstable, Beds, LU6 3HR. Tel (01582) 471700. (*Body kits, lightbrows*)

Coventry Peugeot Specialists, Unit A7, Wolston Business Park, Main Street, Wolston, Coventry, CV8 3LL. Tel (01203) 545995. (*New and secondhand parts, fitting and servicing*)

Dimma UK, Avondale, Oakmere, Cheshire. Tel (01606) 889472. (*Wide-body kits, fuel cap covers*)

Eccles Peugeot, Craven House, Holywell Road, Kingsley Industrial Estate, Kingsley, near Pontefract, WF9 5JB. Tel (01977) 614567. (*New and used spare parts*)

Elite Tyres and Wheels, 136-138 New Road, Rainham, Essex, RM13 8DE. Tel (01708) 525577. (*Exhausts, suspension kits, air filters, alloy wheels and tyres*)

Esquiss Autos, Route de Foujoin, 37210 Vernou s/Brenne, France. Tel (00 33) 47 52 03 27. (*Manufacturers of body styling kits*)

Falkland Performance Centre, Unit 6, Woodgate Way North, Eastfield Industrial Estate, Glenrothes, Falkland, KY7 4PE. Tel (01592) 773677. (*Distributor for Magnex exhausts, Superchips dealer and Bosch servicing agent*)

Fibresports, 34-36 Bowlers Croft, Cranes Industrial Estate, Basildon, Essex, SS14 3ED. Tel (01268) 527331. Fax (01268) 282273. (*Body kits*)

GGB Engineering, 98 White Hart Lane, London, N22 5SG. Tel (0181) 888 2354. (*Tarox brake discs*)

Image and Identity, 1,2 & 3 The Barn, Hilltop Business Park, Devizes Road, Salisbury, Wiltshire, SP3 4UF. Tel (01722) 338855. Fax (01722) 421400. (*Carpet mats*)

International Spare Parts Ltd, Hassop Road, Rear of 219 Cricklewood Broadway, London, NW2 6RX. Tel (0181) 450 0488. Fax (0181) 208 2903. (*Suppliers of Gutmann body styling kits, Brembo brake components and SplitFire performance spark plugs*)

Janspeed Engineering Ltd, Castle Road, Salisbury, Wilts, SP1 3SQ. Tel (01722) 321833. (*Exhausts*)

Jetex Exhausts Ltd, Unit 4, Avenue Farm, Stratford-upon-Avon, Warwickshire, CV37 0HR. Tel (01789) 298989. Fax (01789) 414463. (*Performance exhausts and air filters*)

L A D Motorsport, Whitefield Place, Morecambe, Lancs, LA3 3EA. Tel (01524) 62748. (*Peugeot tuning specialist*)

Magnex Performance Exhausts, Birchwood Way, Coates Park Industrial Estate, Somercotes, Derbyshire, DE55 4QQ. Tel (01773) 831999. (*Stainless steel exhausts*)

Merseyspeed, 227 Warbreck Moor, Aintree, Liverpool, L9 0HU. Tel (0151) 523 1982 or (0151) 525 9954. (*Performance parts – suspension kits, splitters, induction kits, twin headlamp conversions, power boost valves*)

Motomex Peugeot Specialist, Industrial Unit 2/3, Brockhampton Lane, Havant, Hampshire, PO9 1JT. Tel (01705) 470224. (*Servicing*)

Oselli Engineering, Ferry Hinksey Road, Oxford, Oxon, OX2 0BY. Tel (01865) 248100. (*Servicing, rolling-road tuning*)

Pemberton Tyres, 20 Chapel Street, Pemberton, Wigan. Tel (01942) 222413. (*Alloy wheels, suspension, exhausts and air filters*)

Peter Maiden Components, Bodymoor Green Farm, Coventry Road, Kingsbury, North Warwickshire. Tel (01827) 874488. (*Performance parts and styling kits*)

Peugeot Ecosse, 189 Corbiehall, Bo'Ness, Central Scotland, EH51 0AX. Tel (01506) 516106. (*Parts, engine conversions, foreign bodykits and advice*)

Peugeot Spares, Wear Bridge Road Colliery Yard, Sacriston, Tyne & Wear, DH7 6AB. Tel (0191) 371 0201. (*Secondhand spare parts*)

Prima Racing, Sandiacre Road, Stapleford, Nottingham, NG9 8EX. Tel (0115) 949 1903. Fax (0115) 949 1838. (*Scorpion exhausts, spoilers and headlamp conversions*)

PSG, Unit 2, Riverside Court, Westminster Industrial Estate, Measham, Derbyshire, DE12 7DS. Tel (01530) 271139. (*Postert Tuning body styling kits from Germany*)

Pug Parts, Unit 2, Gateway Close, Parkgate, Rotherham, South Yorks, S62 6LJ. Tel (01709) 528811. (*New and used spare parts, repairs and servicing*)

Richard Longman, 5 Airfield Road, Airfield Way Industrial Estate, Christchurch, Dorset. Tel (01202) 486569. (*Rolling road and tuning, engine preparation*)

Shenpar Competitions, 1 Potter Street, Melbourne, Derbyshire. Tel (01332) 862901 (*Fast road conversions, rally preparation, servicing*)

Skip Brown Cars, Ridley Green, Tarporley, Cheshire, CW6 9RY. Tel (01829) 720492. (*Rally preparation, engine building and fast road tuning*)

Spax Ltd, Telford Road Industrial Estate, Bicester, Oxon, OX6 0UU. Tel (01869) 244771. (*Suspension kits*)

Storm Autos, Unit 3, West End Industrial Estate, Witney, Oxon, OX8 6NG. Tel (01993) 771190. Fax (01993) 706008. (*Servicing, rally preparation, spare parts*)

Superchips Ltd, 2-12 The Homestall, Buckingham Industrial Park, Buckingham, Bucks, MK18 1XJ. Tel (01280) 816781. (*Modified ECUs*)

Superspeed, 27 Corstorphine Road, Edinburgh, EH12 7AY. Tel (0131) 316 4200. (*Musketier Exclusiv body styling kits*)

Turbo Technics Ltd, 17 Galowhill Road, Brackmills, Northampton, NN4 0EE. Tel (01604) 764005. (*Turbocharged conversions*)

Van Aaken Developments Ltd, Jigs Lane North, Bracknell, RG42 3DH. Tel (01344) 303999. Fax (01344) 303888. (*Tuning, performance parts, tuning for turbo diesels*)

Performance figures for sporting 205s

In keeping with the policy established with the first *Collector's Guide* in 1978 and maintained ever since, the author has sought the most highly respected sources for accurate performance figures, namely the weekly journals *Autocar* and *Motor*, who have since merged to become one magazine, and to the editor of which grateful thanks are extended. Where figures are not available, the manufacturer's figures are substituted and indicated with an asterisk.

Model	1.4 GT	1.6 GTI	1.6 GTI	1.6 CTI	1.9 GTI	Turbo 16	Turbo 16 E1	Turbo 16 E2
Engine capacity	1360cc	1580cc	1580cc	1580cc	1905cc	1775cc	1775cc	1775cc
Maximum power	80bhp	105bhp	115bhp	115bhp	130bhp	200bhp	n/a	n/a
Maximum speed	105mph	116mph	122mph	116mph	127mph*	130mph	n/a	n/a
Acceleration (sec)								
0-30mph	3.6	3.1	3.1	3.0	2.9	2.5	1.6	1.3
0-40mph	5.4	4.6	4.7	4.7	4.1	3.9	2.2	1.9
0-50mph	8.0	6.4	6.5	6.5	5.9	5.3	3.2	2.4
0-60mph	11.3	8.7	8.7	8.9	7.8	7.8	4.3	3.3
0-70mph	15.8	11.5	11.3	11.8	10.8	10.0	5.2	4.2
0-80mph	22.6	15.3	14.8	15.6	13.7	12.6	6.3	5.3
0-90mph	36.6	20.6	19.5	20.8	18.2	16.4	7.9	6.4
0-100mph	n/a	27.5	26.6	29.7	23.8	21.7	9.4	8.0
Standing ¼-mile	17.9	16.8	17.4	17.5	16.6	15.6	12.6	n/a
Acceleration in top gear								
20-40mph	12.6	9.2	9.4	10.0	7.6	25.6	n/a	n/a
30-50mph	12.1	8.5	9.1	9.1	8.1	13.4	n/a	n/a
40-60mph	12.0	8.2	9.7	9.7	8.1	13.4	5.4	n/a
50-70mph	13.8	9.2	10.0	10.6	8.7	13.4	3.0	n/a
60-80mph	17.4	10.9	11.2	11.9	9.6	13.4	2.3	n/a
70-90mph	28.1	12.5	13.3	14.8	11.3	13.6	2.3	n/a
80-100mph	n/a	15.6	16.1	20.0	14.9	15.3	2.7	n/a
Overall mpg	35.4	31.3	29.9	30.7	28.1	27.1	n/a	n/a
Tested by	*Autocar*	*Motor*	*Autocar*	*Autocar*	*Autocar*	*Autocar*	*Autocar*	*Autocar*
Test weight	1828	1948	1953	2067	2006	2436	n/a	n/a
Test published	28.7.84	7.4.84	3.9.86	3.9.86	21.1.87	23.6.84	21.8.85	10.86